THE VIETNAM WAR

Barbara Diggs

Illustrated by Sam Carbaugh

Nomad Press
A division of Nomad Communications
10 9 8 7 6 5 4 3 2 1

This book was manufactured by Versa Press
East Peoria, Illinois
May 2018, Job # J17-12587

ISBN Softcover: 978-1-61930-660-8
ISBN Hardcover: 978-1-61930-658-5

Educational Consultant, Marla Conn

Questions regarding the ordering of this book should be addressed to
Nomad Press
2456 Christian St.
White River Junction, VT 05001
www.nomadpress.net

Printed in the United States.

Titles in the Inquire & Investigate
Great Events of the Twentieth Century set

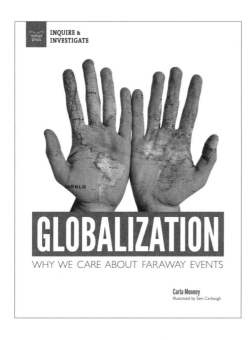

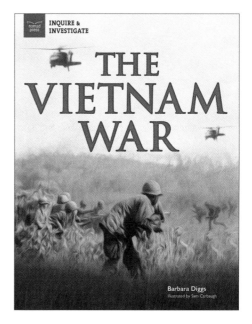

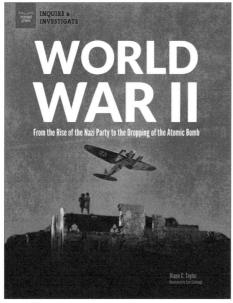

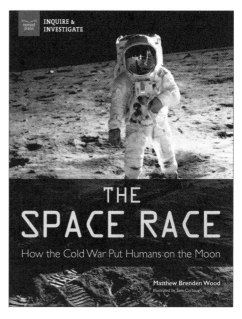

You can use a smartphone or tablet app to scan the QR codes and explore more! Cover up neighboring QR codes to make sure you're scanning the right one. You can find a list of URLs on the Resources page.

If the QR code doesn't work, try searching the internet with the Keyword Prompts to find other helpful sources.

 Vietnam War

What are source notes?

In this book, you'll find small numbers at the end of some paragraphs. These numbers indicate that you can find source notes for that section in the back of the book. Source notes tell readers where the writer got their information. This might be a news article, a book, or another kind of media. Source notes are a way to know that what you are reading is true information that other people have verified. They can also lead you to more places where you can explore a topic that you're curious about!

Contents

Glossary ▼ Resources ▼ Index

TIMELINE

Circa 3000 BCE..... The first-known settlers live in what would become northern Vietnam.

208 BCE............... Chinese General Trieu Da forms the Kingdom of Nam Viet.

111 BCE............... Nam Viet falls under Chinese rule for the next 1,000 years.

938 CE................. The Viet people overthrow the Chinese at the Battle of Bach Dang.

1613.................... Occasional civil war occurs between northern and southern Viet people.

1700s.................. European colonization spreads across Southeast Asia.

1802.................... Emperor Nguyen Anh reunifies the country, calling it "Viet Nam."

1858.................... France attacks the Vietnamese port of Da Nang in retaliation for the persecution of French Catholic priests.

1862.................... The French take control of Saigon through the Treaty of Saigon.

1890.................... Ho Chi Minh is born.

1893.................... The French divide Vietnam into three sectors, part of French Indochina.

1930.................... Ho Chi Minh founds the Vietnamese Communist Party.

1940.................... The Japanese invade Vietnam during World War II.

1941.................... Ho Chi Minh establishes the Viet Minh.

1945.................... The Viet Minh seize control of Hanoi from the Japanese. Ho Chi Minh declares Vietnam independent.

December 1946.... The French-Indochina War begins.

July 1950............. President Harry S. Truman authorizes sending $15 million to aid the French military.

1954.................... The Viet Minh overcome the French at the Battle of Dien Bien Phu. The Geneva Accords are established, dividing Vietnam into North and South at the seventeenth parallel.

1955.................... Prime Minister Ngo Dinh Diem becomes president of South Vietnam. President Dwight D. Eisenhower sends hundreds of U.S. military advisors to South Vietnam to train and strengthen the South Vietnam military and government.

1959.................... Ho Chi Minh declares a "People's War" to unite all of Vietnam. North Vietnam begins widening the Ho Chi Minh Trail for sending supplies and troops to the South.

December 1960.... The National Liberation Front is formed in South Vietnam. Members are unofficially called "Vietcong."

January 1961........ John F. Kennedy is inaugurated as the 35th U.S. president.

November 1963.... President Diem is overthrown and killed. President Kennedy is assassinated. Lyndon B. Johnson becomes president of the United States.

August 1964......... North Vietnam torpedo boats fire on the USS *Maddox* in the Gulf of Tonkin. The U.S. Congress passes the Gulf of Tonkin Resolution, granting the president broad powers to use military force in Indochina.

November 1964–

February 1965...... The Vietcong stage multiple guerrilla attacks on U.S. military bases and the South Vietnamese Army.

March 1965 .... The first U.S. combat troops arrive in South Vietnam. Protests begin at American universities.

August 1965......... Operation Starlite provides the first decisive victory for U.S. troops in Vietnam.

November 1965.... An antiwar rally of 35,000 people takes place in Washington, DC.

1967...................... Support for the war drops as 11,153 U.S. troops die in Vietnam.

January 1968........ The North Vietnamese launch the Tet Offensive.

March 1968 .... President Johnson announces he won't run for reelection and starts negotiations with North Vietnam.

January 1969........ Richard Nixon is sworn in as the 37th U.S. president.

August 1969......... The United States begins to withdraw troops.

September 1969.... Ho Chi Minh dies.

November 1969.... The public learns of the My Lai Massacre. The largest antiwar protest to date occurs with 500,000 marching on Washington, DC.

February 1970...... U.S. National Security Advisor Henry Kissinger begins secret negotiations with diplomat Le Duc Tho of North Vietnam.

Spring 1970.......... President Nixon announces the Cambodia invasion. The Kent State shootings occur.

June 1971............. Excerpts from the Pentagon Papers are published in *The New York Times*.

January 1973........ The Paris Peace Accords is signed.

March 1973 .... U.S. prisoners of war are released and the last U.S. combat troops leave Vietnam.

July 1973.............. Congress votes to end all military activity in Indochina.

August 1974 .... Nixon resigns as president. Gerald Ford becomes president, the sixth to deal with the Vietnam conflict.

April 1975............. Communist troops capture Saigon. South Vietnam surrenders. Saigon is renamed Ho Chi Minh City.

1977...................... President Jimmy Carter pardons all draft evaders.

1982...................... The Vietnam Memorial is unveiled in Washington, DC.

1994...................... President Bill Clinton restores diplomatic relations with Vietnam.

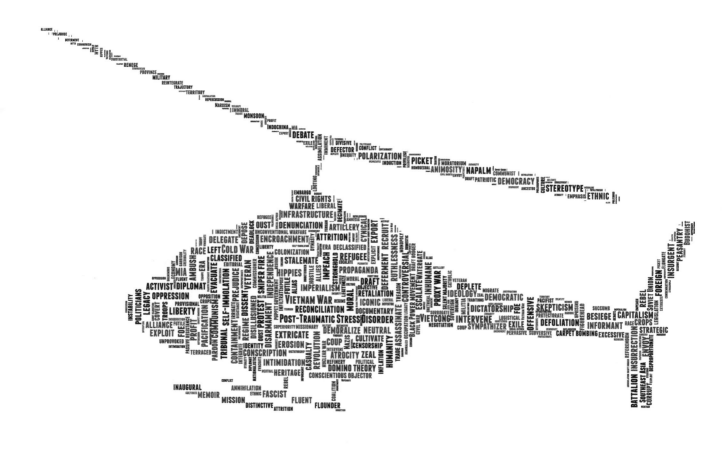

Introduction ▶

What Was the Vietnam War?

Why did the United States get involved with a war between North and South Vietnam?

There were many reasons for the United States to enter a war so far from home, but mainly it was to contain the spread of communism and indirectly engage the Soviet Union.

The Vietnam War was a long and brutal conflict in which communist North Vietnam sought to bring South Vietnam under unified rule. The United States, fearing the spread of communism, stepped in to help South Vietnam resist. Beginning slowly in 1955, the war mushroomed into a conflict of startling proportions. More than 58,000 American troops died, along with an estimated 3 million Vietnamese soldiers and civilians.

Ultimately, after years of fruitless combat and escalating public opposition, the United States withdrew its troops from the conflict in 1973. South Vietnam fell to communism two years later. The war is considered to be a major defeat of the United States.

The Vietnam War stands out in American history for many reasons, but particularly because public opinion about the war was so sharply divided. It remains a controversial and emotional topic for many people even today.

The war left a shocked nation searching for answers to complicated and painful questions. Was the United States right to intervene in the war? Should it have stayed in Vietnam longer? Should it have gotten out sooner? How did the war go so wrong? Whose fault was it? Politicians? The military? The media? The American public?

People still hotly debate many of these questions today—there are no simple answers. The one thing most people agree on is that the Vietnam War was very different from almost any other conflict that the United States had experienced. In fact, for many Americans, the war was more than a military conflict. It was a symbol of an era in which America lost its innocence, and changed how Americans saw themselves and their place in the world.

AN UNCONVENTIONAL WAR

What, exactly, made the Vietnam War so unusual? A mind-bending number of things. It was the United States' longest war at that time. It was the U.S. military's first significant experience with the ruthlessness of guerrilla warfare.

This was the first time Americans watched war unfold on their television sets. It was the first time the military had racially mixed battalions right from the outset. And it was the subject of a massive anti-war protest movement that defined a generation, created a deep rift in the nation, and profoundly impacted both the course of the war and American culture.

PRIMARY SOURCES

Primary sources come from people who were eyewitnesses to events. They might write about the event, take pictures, post short messages to social media or blogs, or record the event for radio or video. The photographs in this book are primary sources, taken at the time of the event. Paintings of events are usually not primary sources, since they are often painted long after the event took place. What other primary sources can you find? Why are primary sources important? Do you learn differently from primary sources than from secondary sources, which come from people who did not directly experience the event?

PS

An infantryman is lowered into a tunnel in Vietnam, 1967

credit: Howard C. Breedlove, SSG, Photographer; U.S. Army Signal Corps

VOCAB LAB

There is a lot of new vocabulary in this book! Turn to the glossary in the back when you come to a word you don't understand. Practice your new vocabulary in the VOCAB LAB activities in each chapter.

The war was also the first to result in widespread erosion of the public's trust in the U.S. government and military. Unlike previous wars, such as World Wars I and II, when most Americans emerged with a sense of pride and moral superiority after the war, many Americans felt disappointed and cynical after the Vietnam War. It was the first war where Americans realized that their government, as in other countries, could deceive its own people.

But right from its beginning, the Vietnam War was distinctive because it was a war within a war. The terrible fight that took place in Vietnam's steamy jungles wasn't simply a domestic dispute between the North and the South. It was a surrogate for a larger, more ominous ideological battle between the United States and the Soviet Union.

HOW IT BEGAN

During the mid-1940s, a decade before the Vietnam War began, the world's political landscape was rapidly changing. Germany's fascist Nazi regime had been defeated in World War II, but the power and influence of the communist Soviet Union was on the rise. Several eastern European countries that had been liberated by the Soviets soon set up communist governments, as did North Korea after being liberated from the Japanese.

Many Western nations, especially the United States, were alarmed by this. They believed both the Soviet Union and communism were dangerous, imminent threats to individual freedom. So when China fell to communism in 1949 and the Vietnamese communists expressed their determination to unify the country under communist rule, the United States vowed to make what the government called the "containment" of communism a high priority.

> The United States threw its support behind the non-communist South Vietnamese government, while the Soviet Union put its weight behind North Vietnam's communist regime.

Because of these relationships, the Vietnam War is known as a proxy war. Neither the United States nor the Soviet Union dared battle each other directly, as each knew such a war could end in nuclear annihilation. Instead, they fought each other through Vietnam's civil struggle. For the United States, the triumph of South Vietnam would mean putting the brakes on communism. It would also be an in-your-face victory over the Soviet Union and all it stood for.

STRATEGY FACT

A proxy war is one in which two or more large, opposing nations avoid direct conflict with each other by using smaller nations to fight their battles for them.

VOCAB LAB

Write down what you think each word means. What root words can you find to help you? What does the context of the word tell you?

communism, containment, cynical, guerrilla warfare, legacy, proxy war, and **regime.**

Compare your definitions with those of your friends or classmates. Did you all come up with the same meanings? Turn to the text and glossary if you need help.

At first, the United States merely supported South Vietnam by giving substantial financial aid and military advice to South Vietnamese forces. But those forces floundered in the face of the strength and cunning of the North Vietnamese army and its allies.

After years of little progress, the United States began sending in American ground combat forces to fight in Vietnam, starting with 3,500 Marines in 1965. And that's when the war began in earnest—as did the cries of protest back home. Both events would impact America with the force of a sledgehammer.

A WAR TO REMEMBER

The Vietnam War was one of the most divisive and iconic conflicts of the modern age. Thousands of books have been written on the subject, from memoirs to novels to military analyses.

Dozens of movies and documentaries have also tried to capture the exceptional atmosphere of the era and the experience of those who served in the war.

This book investigates the causes and trajectory of the Vietnam War, from its earliest roots in nineteenth-century colonization through the final dramatic days of the Fall of Saigon. *The Vietnam War* will help you understand the complexity of the conflict and the unique political and social climates of this era. While emphasis is placed on the role of the United States in the war, hands-on activities and independent study suggestions will give you the opportunity to examine the war from multiple perspectives.

Equally important, this book helps you to appreciate the legacy of the Vietnam War. The effects of this conflict are still seen in American culture and policies today. It's extremely important that present generations continue to study this war to absorb the essential lessons that were learned. Without this knowledge, we are in danger of repeating the same mistakes again and again.

VIETNAM'S PERSPECTIVE

Although the United States, the Soviet Union, and others might have viewed the Vietnam conflict as a proxy war, it wasn't that way for many Vietnamese. For the North Vietnamese and their South Vietnamese allies, the war was a fight for unification of their country and independence from foreign control. In today's Vietnam, the conflict is referred to as the "American War" or the "Resistance War Against America." How do these different names for the same war show different perspectives?

KEY QUESTIONS

- Why do you think the Vietnam War might be a sensitive topic for some people?

- What is the benefit of fighting a proxy war? What are the disadvantages? Do you think proxy wars are more effective than direct wars?

- The Vietnam War was the "first war" in many categories. What are some of the Vietnam War's "firsts" that we now consider standard during wartime?

Inquire & Investigate ▶

CONDUCT AN INTERVIEW

The Vietnam War ended in 1975, which means that many people from this era are still alive today. Despite the numerous books and films that have been made about this war, the best way to get a personal understanding of this period is by speaking with someone who remembers it.

- **Identify someone who lived during the Vietnam era to interview.** If you can't find anyone to interview, try contacting the Veterans of Foreign Wars or the Vietnam Veterans of America.

- **Prepare for the interview by writing a list of questions.** You may want to consider the following questions to get started.

  - How old were you during the war? What were you doing at the time?

  - If you had to describe the Vietnam War era in three words, what words would you use? What do you remember most about the war?

- **During the interview, remember to let the person you're interviewing talk freely.** Be ready to ask follow-up questions based on the information you're given. Also, remember that this can be a delicate topic, especially for those who fought in the war. Be respectful of your interviewee's opinions and experiences.

- **After the interview, write up the interview as an essay or newspaper article.** Consider your audience and decide what to include and what to leave out.

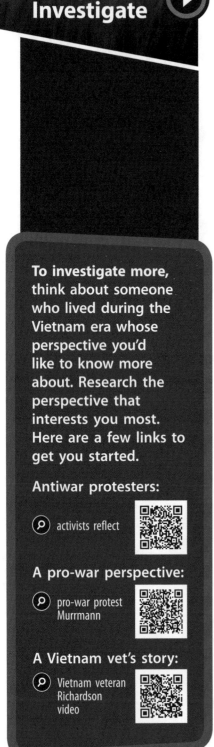

To investigate more, think about someone who lived during the Vietnam era whose perspective you'd like to know more about. Research the perspective that interests you most. Here are a few links to get you started.

Antiwar protesters:

🔍 activists reflect

A pro-war perspective:

🔍 pro-war protest Murrmann

A Vietnam vet's story:

🔍 Vietnam veteran Richardson video

Chapter 1

Vietnam's Revolution Sparks War

THE AMERICANS ARE DOING EXACTLY WHAT THE FRENCH DID.

How did Vietnam's history lead to the Vietnam War?

THE FIRST SETTLERS OF WHAT WOULD BECOME KNOWN AS VIETNAM, THE *LAC VIET*, WERE SAID TO BE DESCENDED FROM A DRAGON AND A CHINESE FAIRY PRINCESS.

IN *208 BCE*, CHINESE GENERAL *TRIEU DA* DECLARED THE NAM VIET KINGDOM TO BE FREE FROM CHINESE RULE. IT REMAINED FREE UNTIL REINVADED.

AFTER MANY EUROPEAN NATIONS STRUGGLED TO CONTROL THE REGION OF VIETNAM, THE FRENCH DOMINATED IN 1862.

THIS WON'T END BADLY.

A history of violence and colonization culminated in a revolution, which lay the foundation for the further revolt that became the Vietnam War.

When many people hear the word "Vietnam," they immediately think—war! But Vietnam has a complex history that dates back thousands of years. To truly understand the reasons behind the Vietnam War, it helps to learn a little about the history of Vietnam and its people.

Vietnam is a long, curving, Southeast Asian country that resembles an elongated S. Extending just below China, the nation runs the length of Laos and Cambodia on its western border and faces the Gulf of Tonkin on its eastern side.

In the north, the country is known for its steep, mystical-looking mountains, rocky islands, and spectacular terraced rice fields. Further south, you'll find coastal plains, steamy jungles, and the famous Mekong Delta, a massive labyrinth of rivers and swamps. The Mekong is sometimes called the rice bowl of Vietnam, because this is where most of the country's rice is produced.

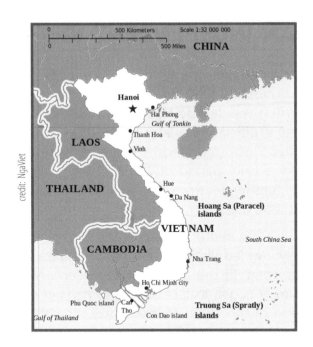

credit: NgaViet

EARLY HISTORY

Around 3000 BCE, people inhabited the area near the Red River Delta, in what is now northern Vietnam. These ancient ancestors of the Vietnamese built a civilization based on cultivating irrigated rice. As centuries passed, many migrated south and settled by the Mekong River.

In 208 BCE, a rebellious Chinese general called Trieu Da (230–137 BCE) declared Au Lac independent from China. He renamed the kingdom Nam Viet (meaning "Viet people of the South") and crowned himself emperor. But 100 years later, China's Han dynasty invaded Nam Viet and returned it to Chinese rule.

For the next 1,000 years, the Chinese ruled over Vietnam, forcing the Vietnamese to adopt Chinese traditions, culture, political philosophies, and language. The Vietnamese resisted assimilation and held on to their sense of national identity, even as the centuries passed.

VIETNAMESE LEGEND

Legend says the Lac Viet descended from the son of a dragon and a Chinese fairy princess, who had 100 sons. The couple's eldest son, Hung Vuong, is said to have founded Vietnam's first dynasty, the Hung dynasty, which lasted 2,861 years. During this period, 18 generations of kings are said to have ruled Van Lang, which is the earliest name for Vietnam, until 258 BCE. In that year, a Chinese prince overtook the kingdom and renamed it Au Lac. While this is mostly myth, it's mingled with truth. Hung Vuong did found the first state of Vietnam, and a line of Hung kings ruled over the kingdom until it was taken over and renamed. Au Lac was what is now northern Vietnam and part of southern China. The Vietnamese call these early settlers the Lac Viet.

AN INDEPENDENT VIETNAM

Independence finally came to Vietnam in 938 CE, after a successful revolt against China's Han dynasty. This uprising was led by Ngo Quyen (897–944), a government official who later became emperor of Vietnam and who founded its first true dynasty. Except for a brief period of Chinese rule in the fifteenth century, Vietnam was a sovereign nation for the next 944 years.

Throughout the centuries, China and Mongolia repeatedly invaded Vietnam, but the Vietnamese fended them off. Then, in the mid-nineteenth century, the French slowly began to take control of parts of Vietnam. By the end of the 1800s, Vietnam was entirely under French authority. And with that, seeds were planted that would eventually grow into the Vietnam War.

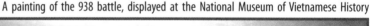
A painting of the 938 battle, displayed at the National Museum of Vietnamese History

VIETNAM FALLS TO THE FRENCH

You might be wondering—how were the French able to take over Vietnam after the country had managed to successfully fight off Chinese invasions for hundreds of years?

The answer lies in what was going on in the rest of Southeast Asia at that time—and in Europe.

From the year 1500 onward, European countries such as Great Britain, Spain, Portugal, and the Netherlands began setting up huge trading posts and settlements in several Southeast Asian nations. They positioned themselves to exploit Southeast Asia's many valuable natural resources, including spices, rubber, cotton, and tea. As centuries passed, the Europeans acquired ever larger amounts of territory in the region, which was then called Indochina, making increasingly greater fortunes from these resources.

A few European countries tried to gain a foothold in Vietnam, but Vietnam's emperors avoided foreign trade. They were deeply mistrustful of foreigners and worried that opening the door to trade with Europeans would lead to imperialism and the destruction of the Vietnamese way of life.

By the mid-1800s, almost all the countries in Southeast Asia had been completely colonized by European nations. The European colonists not only had political, economic, and administrative control of the Asian locals, but many also heavily pressured locals to adopt European religion, language, and culture.

WAR POEMS

Rudyard Kipling's poem "The White Man's Burden" was published in February 1899 in an American magazine. It starts like this.

Take up the White Man's burden—

Send forth the best ye breed—

Go bind your sons to exile

To serve your captives' need;

While the poem referred to the United States' plan to take over the Philippines, it describes the attitudes many Westerners had about colonization. After reading the poem, how would you describe Kipling's view of native civilizations? If a nineteenth-century Vietnamese person wrote a poem in response, what do you think it might say? You can read the rest of the poem at this website.

 White Man's Burden

France was eager to acquire territory in Southeast Asia and was well-positioned to take Vietnam. The French decided to use the Vietnamese persecution of French Catholic priests as a reason to conquer the country. In 1858, when the Emperor Tu Duc (1829–1883) increased persecutions of Catholic missionaries, the French made their move. They attacked the Vietnamese port of Tourane (Da Nang), with the idea of holding it until Vietnam agreed to become a protectorate of France.

The attack turned into a battle that lasted for three years. But at last, Tu Duc gave in to French demands. In 1862, the Treaty of Saigon gave the French the city of Saigon and three southern Vietnamese provinces, along with many other rights and privileges.

Drawing of the taking of the citadel of Saigon from the April 23, 1859, edition of *L'Illustration*

During the next 25 years, the French gradually increased their control over Vietnamese territories.

They stopped referring to the country as Vietnam and divided it into three regions: Cochinchina (southern Vietnam), Amman (central), and Tonkin (north). In 1887, the French declared all three regions, plus Cambodia, to be part of the Indochinese Union. A few years later, Laos was added as well. From then on, the region was collectively referred to as French Indochina. Why do you think France divided and renamed Vietnam?

COLONIZATION AND OPPRESSION

Once the French had control over Vietnam, they quickly imposed a French-style administration on its people. Vietnamese emperors were allowed to remain in place, but they were puppets of the French—they simply did what their new rulers told them to do.

The French were also quick to start taking advantage of Vietnam. Under the direction of Paul Doumer (1857–1932), a former minister of finance in France, the French created monopolies of salt, alcohol, and opium. They also created large rubber plantations and began exporting rice and rubber materials. Most profits from these businesses went to French or wealthy Vietnamese investors. A small percentage was used to build infrastructure such as roads, bridges, and railroads in larger Vietnamese cities. Almost none of it was used to improve the living conditions of the Vietnamese peasantry.

STRATEGY FACT

French people filled virtually all positions of governmental authority, while the Vietnamese were given the most insignificant roles with very low pay.

ROUGH LIVING

Vietnamese peasants suffered terribly under French authority. They were subjected to heavy taxes and many were forced to turn their family land over to the French as payment. Viewed as cheap labor, the peasants were put to work in rice fields, plantations, and refineries, or on public works. Conditions were often poor and most people barely made enough to feed and clothe their families—sometimes they were simply paid in rice.

Terraced rice fields in Vietnam

The Vietnamese were angered by the loss of control of their country and the treatment they received at the hands of the French. Remembering how the Chinese had colonized their country for 10 centuries and how their ancestors had fought it, they organized resistance groups and rebelled against the French. But the French were able to squash all uprisings.

The tide began to turn in 1941, when a new national movement for Vietnamese liberation began to gain momentum. It was led by a man named Ho Chi Minh (1890–1969). He would become the founder of the Vietnamese Communist Party. And it was this person who drove the North Vietnamese to victory in the Vietnam War.

HO CHI MINH AND THE VIET MINH

Ho Chi Minh was born in central Vietnam in 1890. His father was a government official who resigned in protest when the French came to power. Growing up, Ho Chi Minh absorbed his father's nationalistic and anti-colonial sentiment, even as he was educated in French schools in Vietnam.

Ho Chi Minh in 1921

In 1911, Ho Chi Minh left Vietnam to travel all around the world. He lived in New York, London, Paris, Moscow, Thailand, and Canton in China, and is said to have become fluent in the languages of each of those places.

Wherever he went, he studied the political ideologies of each nation. While he was intrigued by ideas of democracy, socialism, and Marxism, he believed that communism would bring the best results for his country. Ho Chi Minh lived in Moscow in 1923, just six years after the Russian Revolution and the establishment of communist rule. He studied communism at Moscow's University of Oriental Workers, determined to bring his own revolution to Vietnam when the timing was right.

That time came in the early 1940s during World War II, when the Japanese invaded Indochina and set up a puppet government in Vietnam. Ho Chi Minh realized that the French were now in a seriously weakened position. Not only had the French grasp on Vietnam been loosened by the Japanese, but France itself had been taken over by Nazi Germany. In May 1941, Ho Chi Minh formed an organization in southern China, near the Vietnam border, called Viet Nam Doc Lap Dong Minh Hoi (Viet Minh), which meant "League for the Independence of Vietnam."

THE AUGUST REVOLUTION

The Viet Minh was both a political movement and a military force. Although the group was rooted in communism, its primary mission was to liberate Vietnam. This was a cause that had broad appeal for Vietnamese across a variety of political and social classes. Ho Chi Minh believed that if the Viet Minh could wrest power from the Japanese in Vietnam, they could also oust the French and form an independent Vietnam.

NGUYEN SINH CUNG

Ho Chi Minh's birth name was Nguyen Sinh Cung. He used multiple aliases throughout his lifetime, but took the name Ho Chi Minh as he began to lead the revolution. The name means "Bringer of Light." Later, during the Vietnam War, both friends and foes often referred to him as Uncle Ho.

STRATEGY FACT

Although Ho Chi Minh traveled for 30 years without returning to Vietnam, he never stopped thinking about how the Vietnamese could successfully revolt against colonial rule.

Ho Chi Minh appointed a revolutionary named Vo Nguyen Giap (1911–2013) to recruit northern Vietnamese village chiefs, local tribespeople, and other Vietnamese citizens to form a guerrilla militia. Meanwhile, Ho Chi Minh traveled in southern China to expand his network of supporters and seek alliances with diplomats of various countries.

By 1943, the Viet Minh was powerful enough to start striking French and Japanese posts in northern Vietnam and liberate several areas from foreign control. Just as the Japanese surrendered to the Allies in August 1945, the Viet Minh called upon the Vietnamese population for a general uprising throughout Vietnam. For 10 days, guerrilla-style insurrections took place all around the country, with the Viet Minh seizing control of the northern city of Hanoi, Vietnam's capital. This uprising is known as the August Revolution.

On September 2, 1945, Ho Chi Minh declared Vietnam an independent country. In a speech before 500,000 Vietnamese citizens in Hanoi, he announced that the Viet Minh would serve as Vietnam's provisional government and that the country would now be called the Democratic Republic of Vietnam.

THE FIRST INDOCHINA WAR

Despite Ho Chi Minh's declaration of independence, the French were not ready to give up control of Vietnam. The northern part of the country was firmly in the grasp of the Viet Minh, but the southern half was in turmoil. In Saigon, Vietnam's largest southern city, the Viet Minh and rival Vietnamese political groups fought with each other and the French for control. With the aid of British troops, the French were able to temporarily pacify the southern region and regain political power.

Meanwhile, in the north, Ho Chi Minh was struggling to get other countries to recognize Vietnam as independent. A month before the August Revolution, the Allied Powers of World War II had agreed during the Potsdam Conference to send Chinese troops to northern Vietnam to flush out the Japanese troops. Chinese troops came, but spent most of their time looting Hanoi.

Ho repeatedly asked for help from U.S. President Harry Truman, but the United States ignored these requests. It was in its interests to stay allied with the French to help rebuild Europe, which was in shambles after World War II, and develop the North American Treaty Organization (NATO). The United States was also increasingly uneasy about the power of the Soviet Union and wanted to contain the expansion of communism. There was little chance the United States would support a communist government.

In early 1946, a desperate Ho Chi Minh agreed to negotiate with the French. He struck a deal in which Vietnam would be considered a free state within the French Union, although 25,000 French troops would be allowed to remain in Vietnam temporarily. But several months later, a French high commissioner reneged on the agreement by declaring the southern part of Vietnam the Republic of Cochinchina and entirely French-controlled.

Full-blown war between the Vietnamese and the French began in December 1946. A month earlier, a French naval ship bombarded the northern port town of Haiphong. They wanted to flush out Vietnamese guerrillas, but ended up killing more than 6,000 Vietnamese, mainly civilians. In response, Vietnamese guerrillas attacked the French in Hanoi a month later. The war was on.

BAO DAI

In 1949, the French installed former Emperor Bao Dai (1913–1997) as the head of South Vietnam. Bao Dai had been a puppet emperor appointed by the Japanese during their occupation of Vietnam, but he abdicated to the Viet Minh when they took control of Hanoi. By returning Bao Dai to an official position, the French hoped to give the impression of an independent Vietnam. But Bao Dai remained little more than a figurehead. Even so, many Western countries, including the United States, officially recognized Bao Dai's false regime.

Ho Chi Minh during the Battle of Dong Khe, 1950

At first, the United States avoided becoming involved in the Indochina War. But when Chinese communists took over mainland China in 1949 and North Korea's communist forces swept into Seoul, South Korea, in 1950, U.S. foreign policy changed.

Fearing the spread of communism throughout Asia, the United States began giving substantial financial support to the French military. Around the same time, both the Soviet Union and communist China officially recognized the Democratic Republic of Vietnam as independent. They began financially supporting and training the Viet Minh and supplying them with arms.

BATTLE OF DIEN BIEN PHU

For years, the two sides were locked in a violent stalemate. The French had more powerful weapons and equipment than the Viet Minh, but the Vietnamese force was larger and more adept at fighting on their home terrain of mountains and jungles. What's more, once China and the Soviet Union began supplying the Viet Minh with arms, the quality of their weapons improved, and they became even more powerful.

The war came to a dramatic conclusion in March 1954 at the battle of Dien Bien Phu. French troops created a garrison at the bottom of an isolated jungle valley to protect France's main air strip. After learning of their plans, General Giap's soldiers hauled 200 pieces of major artillery up the mountains and concealed them in caves above the valley. A showdown took place, but the French were at a strategic disadvantage and massively outnumbered—10,000 Frenchmen to 45,000 Viet Minh.

From their mountain position, the Viet Minh crippled the French airstrip and strongholds, and slowly approached and surrounded the French base. Weakened, the French continued to fight, but it was clear the end was near. On May 7, 1954, the Viet Minh stormed the French base, taking several thousand French troops as prisoners. For the French, it was enough.

The eight-year war was over. And the French colonization of Vietnam was over, too.

Can you think of any other advantages the Vietnamese forces had over the French? Consider the motivations of the French fighters compared to the motivations of the Vietnamese.

STRATEGY FACT

By the war's end, the United States had provided about 3 billion dollars in support of the French, and financed nearly 80 percent of France's war supplies.

A French soldier in the Red River Delta, between Haiphong and Hanoi, 1954

VOCAB LAB

Write down what you think each word means. What root words can you find to help you? What does the context of the word tell you?

assimilation, **democracy**, **exploit**, **imperialism**, **monopoly**, **nationalistic**, **national identity**, **protectorate**, **puppet government**, **revolution**, **socialism**, **sovereign**, and **stalemate**.

Compare your definitions with those of your friends or classmates. Did you all come up with the same meanings? Turn to the text and glossary if you need help.

DECISIONS OF 1954

The Indochina war effectively ended with the battle at Dien Bien Phu. But many wondered: Who would govern Vietnam? Should Vietnam be unified or left divided? When would each side withdraw its troops?

On May 8, 1954, delegates from the Democratic Republic of Vietnam (the future North Vietnam), France, the People's Republic of China, the Soviet Union, Laos, Cambodia, the State of Vietnam (the future South Vietnam), and the United States met in Geneva, Switzerland, to determine how to resolve these problems.

The conference was tense. Every nation wanted to protect its own interests and had different ideas about what should happen.

The Democratic Republic of Vietnam wanted a unified Vietnam under a communist government. China, newly communist and worried about potential American intervention, said it didn't object to a divided Vietnam with a communist north and non-communist south. France mainly wanted to ensure a cease-fire. The United States was adamantly opposed to any part of Vietnam being under communist control.

With all this in mind, several points were finally agreed upon in July 1954.

- Vietnam would be an independent nation, but would be temporarily divided into two countries at the seventeenth parallel.

- The Viet Minh would control the North, while Bao Dai's government would control the South.

- Nationwide elections would occur within two years to decide which political system would govern the entire country.

The United States and the newly created South Vietnam were extremely dissatisfied with this outcome and neither delegate signed the agreement. They were concerned that Ho Chi Minh might win the election, which could kick off a wave of communism throughout Asia.

In the next chapter, we'll learn exactly why the United States feared and loathed communism so much—and how this fear and loathing drove the country to become increasingly involved in Vietnam.

KEY QUESTIONS

- Are there any colonized countries existing in the world today? What do you think are the feelings and opinions of people living in a colonized country?

- In what ways did Vietnam's history play a role in its reaction toward French colonization?

- Do you think the United States regretted helping Ho Chi Minh during World War II? Do you think it regretted not helping him during the Indochina War? Why or why not?

Ho Chi Minh's Declaration of Independence

🔍 Vietnam Declaration

The U.S. Declaration of Independence

🔍 Declaration of Independence

To investigate more, imagine that your country is taken over by another and you want to appeal to a third country for help. Which country do you think you'd reach out to? Why? What would you say? Write a letter.

WHAT IS INDEPENDENCE?

Despite being a communist, Ho Chi Minh was clearly influenced by the history and political philosophy of the United States, itself a former colony. When he gave his declaration of independence speech to North Vietnamese citizens on September 2, 1945, he started it by quoting from the American Declaration of Independence.

- **Read a translation of Ho Chi Minh's declaration of independence and the U.S. Declaration of Independence.**

  - How are the two declarations similar? How are they different?

  - How would you describe the tone of each declaration? What do you think accounts for any difference in tone between the two?

- **Why do you think Ho Chi Minh quoted the U.S. Declaration of Independence?** Do you think he might have had any political motivations in doing so? If so, what were they?

- **During the First Indochina War, Ho Chi Minh wrote several letters and telegrams to President Harry Truman, asking for help in establishing Vietnam's independence.** Read one telegram at this website, then answer the following questions.

  🔍 Ho Chi Minh telegram

  - What specific words does Ho Chi Minh use in this telegram to appeal to the United States?

  - Why do you think he kept trying to appeal to the United States, even after he was ignored?

Chapter 2

The Cold War Heats Up the Conflict

MR. PRESIDENT, THERE IS A DANGER COMMUNISM COULD SPREAD IN ASIA.

What influence did the fear of communism have on the government of the United States?

THE STRUGGLE OF *HO CHI MINH* AGAINST THE FRENCH HELPED PAVE THE ROAD TO THE VIETNAM WAR. THE UNITED STATES FEARED HIS VICTORY WOULD LEAD TO A FULLY COMMUNIST VIETNAM.

GENTLEMEN, COMMUNISM IS SPREADING LIKE A DISEASE IN ASIA. FIRST, THE CONFLICT ON THE KOREAN CONTINENT. NOW, IT SEEMS LIKE IT WILL SWEEP THROUGH THE SOUTHEAST. WE MUST STOP IT COLD.

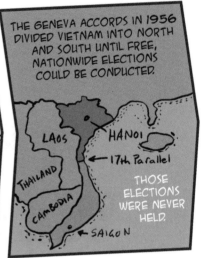

THE GENEVA ACCORDS IN 1956 DIVIDED VIETNAM INTO NORTH AND SOUTH UNTIL FREE, NATIONWIDE ELECTIONS COULD BE CONDUCTED.

LAOS
HANOI
THAILAND
← 17th Parallel
CAMBODIA
THOSE ELECTIONS WERE NEVER HELD.
← SAIGON

With communist governments in the Soviet Union, Eastern Europe, and China, the United States saw the spread of communism as a threat to its own democratic and capitalist way of life.

Vietnam's struggle for independence from the French was one road that led to the Vietnam War. The second road was the tense ideological standoff between the United States and the Soviet Union known as the Cold War.

Although the Cold War era began in the 1940s, the United States and the Soviet Union had been wary of one another since the Russian Revolution in 1917. This is when rebels overthrew the Russian monarch and created the totalitarian communist government of the Soviet Union.

In a communist country, the government completely controls the economy, including the production and distribution of goods. All citizens are totally subservient to the authority of the government. The United States hated both communism and totalitarianism, finding such ideologies hostile to economic and personal freedom.

The Soviets equally despised the U.S. economic system, capitalism. In a capitalist system, private businesses, not the government, decide what to produce and distribute. The Soviets believed the system unfairly favored the wealthy and didn't ensure that everyone's basic needs were met. Both the United States and the Soviet Union believed that their system was the best, and the other system was evil.

Despite the animosity between the two nations, both countries put aside their differences to become allies to stop the advancement of the Nazis during World War II. But when the Allies won and the war ended in 1945, the old tensions came right back.

EASTERN EUROPE GOES RED

World War II had left most European counties struggling economically, so the United States, Soviet Union, and Britain had to help re-establish order. Because the Soviet Union had been invaded by the Nazis and suffered the most damage and casualties, it felt it had the right to impose communist dictatorships in the Central and Eastern European nations it had liberated from Nazi occupation. Within four years, Romania, Hungary, Poland, Czechoslovakia, Bulgaria, East Germany, Yugoslavia, and Albania were all communist.

The United States was extremely uneasy about the Soviet Union's new sphere of influence in Eastern Europe. Many U.S. officials believed the Soviet Union was out to conquer and destroy all capitalist and democratic states. They also worried that communism and its ideal of economic equality might appeal to countries that were suffering severe economic hardships because of the war.

STRATEGY FACT

The Cold War arose out of extreme differences between the American and Soviet economic systems and forms of government.

THE "CONTAINMENT" DOCTRINE

Why might communism be attractive to economically struggling countries?

Listen to President Truman's speech to Congress at this website. Do you find his arguments persuasive? Why or why not?

 Truman joint session 1947

Determined to prevent other countries from falling to communism, in March 1947, President Harry S. Truman (1884–1972) requested $400 million from Congress to help the Greek and Turkish governments, which were both struggling with communist rebellions. He argued that the expansion of communism and totalitarianism would put international peace and U.S. national security at risk. The United States therefore had an obligation to contain communism and help "free and independent nations to maintain their freedom."[1]

Truman's speech marked the beginning of a new kind of foreign policy for the United States. Up to then, the United States tried to avoid intervening in foreign affairs during peacetime. Now, it became a major part U.S. foreign policy to intervene in countries at risk of falling to communism.

Not only did the United States send financial aid to Greece and Turkey as Truman requested, it also began an initiative known as the Marshall Plan. This program offered $13 billion in direct aid and loans to Western European countries during the next four years. The money helped them stabilize their economies and strengthen their democracies.

ASIA GOES COMMUNIST

Even as the United States strengthened its stance against communism, this ideology continued to take hold in other parts of the world. In 1949, the 22-year Chinese Civil War ended when China's Communist Party took over mainland China. A year later, North Korea invaded South Korea with the intention of unifying the peninsula under its communist government.

The 1st Marine Division moves through communist China lines during the Battle of Chosin Reservoir, 1950

credit: Corporal Peter McDonald, U.S. Marine Corps

Armed with its new policy of containment, the United States leapt into action. President Truman sent American troops to South Korea to help oust the North Koreans. China sent troops to support the North Korean army, while the Soviet Union provided financial, tactical, and air support. The first military action of the Cold War was underway.

After three years, the Korean War ended in a draw. Although the United States continued to oppose communism, officials didn't want the war to escalate into a direct war with China or Russia, which could trigger a nuclear war. In 1953, the new U.S. president, Dwight Eisenhower (1890–1969), helped broker a peace deal in which Korea would remain divided between communist North Korea and democratic South Korea.

THE LONG TELEGRAM

It was George F. Kennan (1904–2005), U.S. ambassador to Moscow, who first used the word *containment* with respect to stopping the spread of Soviet influence. In 1946, Kennan sent President Truman an 8,000-word missive known as "The Long Telegram" and published anonymously an article urgently calling for the containment of the large threat he believed the Soviets posed to the free world. He wrote, "This would of itself warrant the United States entering with reasonable confidence upon a policy of firm containment, designed to confront the Russians with unalterable counter-force at every point where they show of encroaching upon the interests of a peaceful and stable world."

You can read the whole article at this website.

 Kennan containment article

Vietnam refugees leaving Haiphong, August 1954

credit: PH1 H.S. Hemphill, U.S. Navy

STRATEGY FACT

The late 1940s and '50s is known as the second Red Scare. The first Red Scare occurred just after World War I, when Russia turned to communism. It is called red because of the color red in the Soviet flag.

The situation in Vietnam, however, remained uncertain. This was a concern for U.S. officials. These worries skyrocketed in April 1954, when the Viet Minh were poised to defeat the French army at the battle of Dien Bien Phu. It looked as if the communists might win all of Vietnam.

This was an outcome that the United States couldn't bear to consider.

THE RED SCARE

As the Korean War came to an end and Vietnam became more of a worry, the United States reached a full-blown panic about communism. For decades, there had been a fear, with some justification, that Soviet spies had secretly infiltrated the U.S. federal government. As communism spread across Eastern Europe and Asia in the late 1940s, this fear blossomed into hysteria.

Starting in 1947, U.S. law required federal government employees to be analyzed to assess their faithfulness to the United States. The FBI began keeping many left-leaning organizations under strict surveillance through wiretaps and infiltration. The House Un-American Activities Committee, a committee of the U.S. House of Representatives, grilled thousands of American citizens suspected of being communists or communist sympathizers. The committee asked about their political beliefs and pressured them to name others who might be engaged in what it called subversive, un-American activities.

It was in this atmosphere of fear and suspicion that U.S. officials watched the French army falter at Dien Bien Phu. On April 7, 1954, President Eisenhower held a news conference to explain the gravity of the situation. He famously explained that if the French lost to Ho Chi Minh's forces, the entire southeast Asia region could fall to communism like "dominoes."[2]

A month later, the French finally succumbed to North Vietnam. Three months later, the Geneva Accords agreed to temporarily divide Vietnam into North and South until nationwide elections were held in 1956.

McCARTHYISM

The second Red Scare is almost synonymous with the term McCarthyism. U.S. Senator Joseph McCarthy (1908–1957) made sweeping accusations of rampant communism inside the U.S. government without any evidence. He became the most prominent politician of the Red Scare era, greatly fanning the flames of paranoia and fear with his denunciations. McCarthyism is now a negative term that refers to accusations of disloyalty, treason, or subversion made with weak or unreliable evidence. Can you find examples of McCarthyism in American society today?

The Geneva Accords allowed Vietnamese citizens 300 days to migrate between the North and the South before the country was officially divided at the seventeenth parallel. Between 700,000 and 1 million Vietnamese in the north fled south, fearing the communist government. From 1954 to 1955, the U.S. Navy provided ships to help approximately 310,000 people move. Although the United States had humanitarian motives, it had political ones as well. Many of the people who moved were Catholics who could help bolster support for South Vietnam's leader, Ngo Dinh Diem, who was also a Catholic. In contrast, only a few thousand communist supporters moved from south to north. Some communists remained in the South to await instructions from the North.

The Eisenhower administration was unhappy with this result. Officials knew that if the United States was going to commit to its policy of containment, it would have to help South Vietnam fight against the communist North. The administration decided the United States' best hope was to throw its support behind South Vietnam's prime minister, Ngo Dinh Diem (1901–1963).

This relationship would end in disaster.

PRESIDENT NGO DINH DIEM

Ngo Dinh Diem was a Vietnamese civil servant who had been appointed prime minister of South Vietnam by Bao Dai, South Vietnam's head of state, in 1954. In some ways, Diem seemed the perfect leader to develop a strong, democratic state. He wanted an independent Vietnam, but was fiercely anti-communist. He was familiar with Western ways— he attended French Catholic school in Vietnam and even lived in New Jersey for a few years.

But although Diem spoke of democracy and self-determination, he had the old-fashioned, authoritarian style of a Vietnamese emperor. Despite his exposure to American-style politics, he either did not understand the fundamentals of democracy or didn't care. Many in South Vietnam deeply opposed him.

In 1955, 15 months after becoming prime minister, Diem called for a referendum to depose Bao Dai and make himself president of South Vietnam. But this election was hardly an exercise in democracy. Voters were intimidated at the polling stations and Diem won by hundreds of thousands more votes than there were registered voters.

Nonetheless, Diem declared victory and renamed the country the Republic of Vietnam.

Closing its eyes to Diem's shortcomings, the Eisenhower administration tried to help Diem create a stable government and strong military. In November 1955, President Eisenhower sent hundreds of U.S. military advisors to help train the Army of the Republic of Vietnam (ARVN) and funneled millions of dollars to the South Vietnam government.

A year later, when Diem refused to honor the Geneva Accords' requirements to hold nationwide elections, Eisenhower enthusiastically supported him. Eisenhower was certain that if the elections took place, Ho Chi Minh would easily beat the unpopular Diem. This was a case in which the outcome seemed to justify the dishonorable methods. But was it worth it?

Diem's rule was corrupt and violent, creating resentment among southern peasants. Support for communism surged. Former Viet Minh agents living in the South began to assassinate Diem officials and call upon the North for help.

BIRTH OF THE VIETCONG

While Diem was struggling with his Saigon government, Ho Chi Minh had problems of his own in Hanoi.

The Viet Minh had changed its name to Lao Dong (the Vietnamese Workers Party), and had become a distinctly communist organization. In 1955, Ho instituted a land reform program, forcing landowners to turn over their property to the state. This resulted in the torture and murder of thousands of landowners by tribunals, which were determined to punish citizens simply for owning land. Despite the massacre, Ho's supporters largely forgave him after he acknowledged that using violence instead of persuasion had been a mistake.

THE HO CHI MINH TRAIL

To slip into South Vietnam unnoticed, the North Vietnamese used a path that would later become an important feature in the Vietnam War—the Ho Chi Minh Trail. More than 620 miles long, it passed through the countries of Laos and Cambodia. This trail was a tangled network of mountain and jungle paths shrouded by dense canopies of foliage. It had to be widened so that North Vietnamese troops, as well as weapons and supplies provided by the Soviets and Chinese, could reach the South more easily. North Vietnam used the trail throughout the Vietnam War, despite it being repeatedly bombed by U.S. forces.

SOUTHERN LAOS
Ho Chi Minh Trail
1967

Infiltration Trail Areas   Sihanouk Trail

Roads and
Feeder Routes   Other Routes

0   25   50   75 Miles
0   25   50   75 Kilometers

As North Vietnam grew more stable, Ho's government realized that national elections would never be held. That meant it could focus attention on recapturing the South. In May 1959, North Vietnam sent a group of soldiers, known as Group 559, to secretly assess the situation and bring supplies and arms to the South. Group 559 reported that communists in the South were ready for war, and had begun to take matters into their own hands.

Although North Vietnam didn't feel ready to take political control of the South, it agreed that southern communists should continue assassinating Diem's local officials, which they did with merciless zeal. Between 1959 and 1961, southern insurgents killed as many as 4,000 officials each year.

The insurgents of the South were officially called the People's Armed Forces of Liberation. Diem's forces, however, referred to them as Vietcong, which meant "Vietnamese communists." The name was meant to be insulting, but the Vietcong embraced it. In December 1960, the North Vietnam government announced the creation of the National Liberation Front (NLF) to coordinate the overthrow of the Diem government and to direct the actions of the Vietcong.

JOHN F. KENNEDY TAKES CHARGE

As Vietcong attacks in South Vietnam increased in the early 1960s, Cold War tensions were as strong as ever. Cuba had undergone a communist revolution in 1959. Laos, which shared a border with Vietnam, was in the midst of a civil war with communist insurgents. And Soviet Prime Minister Nikita Khrushchev (1894–1971) had chillingly announced that the Soviet Union would support any wars of liberation worldwide. Why would this cause anxiety for the American government?

In January 1961, a young senator named John F. Kennedy (1917–1963) became the 35th U.S. president. His inaugural speech was one of peace, hope, and unity, but was also a declaration of his commitment—and the American responsibility—to containing communism. But when it came to deciding how to do so, there was division in his administration, particularly with respect to Vietnam.

Vietnamese paratroopers jump from U.S. Air Force Fairchild C-123B Provider transports in the initial air assault wave against the Vietcong in South Vietnam, March 1963.

credit: U.S. Army

Pacification is a method of making a potentially rebellious population peaceful.

Some of President Kennedy's advisors thought that a show of force with U.S. combat troops would bring a quick end to the Vietnam conflict. Kennedy, however, hoped to help South Vietnam by improving its political, economic, and military structures without direct help from American troops. He and other officials who supported such nation-building believed that if the South Vietnamese could see the benefits of democracy and capitalism, it would motivate them to fight communism.

Kennedy increased the number of U.S. military advisors in Vietnam from about 700 in 1961 to 16,000 by 1963. He also continued to quietly send hundreds of millions of dollars to support the South Vietnam military, and supplied the country with helicopters, planes, and ships.

At the same time, he and his advisors struggled to come up with ways to make Diem a more likeable president. This was an uphill battle.

Diem had held another election in 1959, but it was as corrupt as the first. He refused to push his much-disliked brother and sister-in-law out of his political circle, despite urgings from both the United States and his own generals. What's more, he seemed unable to grasp that improving the economic condition of the peasants could be a stronger defense against communism than trying to capture or kill all the communists in the South.

STRATEGIC HAMLET PROGRAM

Much of the South was riddled with Vietcong by late 1961. They were not only attacking Diem officials, but also recruiting peasants to join them, often through intimidation and terror. Whole villages and territories were under Vietcong control.

In response, the Diem government came up with an initiative called the Strategic Hamlet Program. The goal of this pacification program was to separate peasants from the Vietcong by moving millions of peasants into armed rural communities.

> This would cut off the supply of
> new recruits for the Vietcong.

The Kennedy administration saw this as an opportunity to help educate the peasants and institute social reforms. The hamlets were to have schools, hospitals, and other modern conveniences to make life better for residents. The United States willingly financed the project. Unfortunately, the plan backfired.

The peasants deeply resented being forced to move from their ancestral lands. The hamlets were desolate and surrounded with barbed wire, bamboo spikes, and ditches, all of which the peasants had to construct themselves. They were told they'd be paid to move, but often the money was either late or landed in the pockets of corrupt officials instead.

Moreover, the Vietcong were able to reach the peasants anyway. In the end, the program increased hostility toward Diem. It's believed to have turned many peasants in the hamlets into communist sympathizers, if not actual Vietcong.

Although the Kennedy officials tried to view the situation in Vietnam positively, it was becoming clear that the Vietcong were capturing more and more territory in the South. They were showing themselves difficult to defeat, even in the face of superior weaponry and a greater number of opponents.

The Battle of Ap Bac helped prove this point.

STRATEGY FACT

How would you feel if you were made to move from your home? What other times in history have groups of people been made to leave their homes, presumably for their own safety?

In December 1962, the Vietcong had positioned themselves near Ap Bac, a village southwest of Saigon in the Mekong Delta. With help from American helicopter pilots, the ARVN engaged with the Vietcong. The ARVN had four times as many soldiers as the Vietcong, as well as more artillery and armor. Despite this, the Vietcong lost only three soldiers and managed to shoot down five helicopters and leave 180 ARVN soldiers and three Americans dead.

The Kennedy administration and South Vietnam tried to spin this battle as a victory because the Vietcong abandoned their positions by Ap Bac. But the U.S. media portrayed the battle as a loss. Despite the billions of dollars and time the United States had invested, it seemed that the ARVN was not yet competent enough to successfully fight the Vietcong.

DIEM'S DOWNFALL

In 1963, President Diem was as disliked by his people as ever. That spring, Saigon was overcome with sweeping protests of Diem's terrible treatment of Buddhists. A few Buddhist monks even protested by setting themselves on fire in an act called self-immolation. Diem refused to acknowledge his government's poor treatment of the Buddhists. His prominent sister-in-law made things even worse by mocking the self-immolations.[3]

Diem was also rapidly losing the support of his military generals. In the summer of 1963, these generals approached the U.S. ambassador in Saigon, Henry Cabot Lodge Jr. (1902–1985), to find out how the United States would feel about an overthrow of Diem's regime. Many U.S. officials were fed up with Diem's inflexibility and agreed that he should go.

President Kennedy and the First Lady minutes before he was shot and killed

credit: Victor Hugo King

Confronted with the question, President Kennedy had reservations, but left the decision to Lodge. Lodge believed that Diem was making the United States look bad, and that an overthrow would be in U.S. interests. He gave the green light.

The coup took place on November 1, 1963. Diem and his brother were initially able to slip away, but later, they were caught and brutally murdered. Even though he was expecting the overthrow, President Kennedy was shocked by the news of their deaths.

Just three weeks later, Kennedy himself was assassinated during a trip to Dallas, Texas. As the United States mourned the loss of its leader, the murder of the two central political figures in the Vietnam drama would shift the course of the war once again. The conflict landed squarely in the lap of Kennedy's successor, Lyndon B. Johnson (1908–1973).

In the next chapter, we'll look at how President Johnson pulled the United States deeper into the war.

KEY QUESTIONS

- Do you think the United States, or any country, has a moral obligation to help other countries resolve their domestic disputes? Why or why not?

- Why do you think President Kennedy believed that focusing on improving the lives of the peasants might help fight communism? Do you agree?

- Did the anti-communist activity in the United States violate any American rights or liberties? Why or why not?

Inquire & Investigate

VOCAB LAB

A PEEK AT PROPAGANDA

Anti-communist propaganda helped perpetuate the fear of communism in the United States during the Cold War. Propaganda is the spread of biased or misleading messages to support or damage a particular cause, institution, or group. From the late 1940s through the early 1960s, the U.S. government, universities, and even Hollywood directors produced numerous anti-communist propaganda films and videos. Cartoons were also made with anti-communist messages to target children. You can watch a selection of such propaganda films and videos from the era below.

* **Watch some or all of each video, then complete the following exercise to learn how propaganda works.**

The Red Menace

Anti communist cartoon

How to Spot a Communist

* Identify three images or symbols used to influence the audience.

* Identify three themes used in these films to persuade the audience.

* Were any emotions or prejudices played upon? If so, what were they?

* Did you find any of these films convincing? If so, what made them persuasive?

- **Make a five-minute propaganda video in opposition to a cause you believe in.** As you create it, consider the following.

  - Who is your intended audience?

  - Who are the actors in your video? What physical characteristics, mannerisms, and clothing will help communicate your message?

  - What symbols, images, or themes will help reinforce your point?

  - What background music can help stir emotions?

  - What kind of setting is most effective?

  - What title would best communicate your message?

> To investigate more, name some ideologies that people feel strongly about today. Have you seen propaganda associated with these ideologies? What form did it take? What made it effective? Is there any ideology that you support? If so, can you find propaganda for that ideology? It can take the form of films, books, videos, articles, advertisements, or even memes.

Inquire & Investigate

Chapter 3
Sinking Deeper into Hostilities

THIS IS EAGLE ONE. WE HAVE REACHED HANOI AND WILL BEGIN OUR BOMB RUN.

Why did President Johnson begin bombing Vietnam?

DURING THE 1964 PRESIDENTIAL ELECTION, PRESIDENT JOHNSON WAS IN A BIND. PUBLICALLY, HE CAMPAIGNED FOR PEACE, BUT PRIVATELY, HE KNEW THE U.S. COULDN'T LEAVE VIETNAM.

IF AMERICA LEFT, THE NORTH VIETNAMESE COMMUNISTS WOULD WIN.

AFTER HE WON THE ELECTION, JOHNSON STEADILY INCREASED AMERICAN TROOP NUMBERS... SINKING THE U.S. DEEPER INTO THE WAR.

President Johnson believed that communism would spread from country to country if South Vietnam fell to the Vietcong. He believed the best way to stop it was to gradually increase military pressure on North Vietnam.

President Kennedy's assassination shook the entire nation, but it changed the life of Vice President Lyndon B. Johnson. On November 22, 1963, just hours after Kennedy's death, Johnson was sworn in as president. Two days later, he pledged to continue President Kennedy's policy of providing military and economic support to Vietnam. However, Johnson's policies would go far beyond Kennedy's, escalating the war to heights few could have imagined.

President Johnson was an influential Democratic senator from Texas before he become vice president. His passion lay not in foreign policy, but domestic affairs. It was his goal as president to bring about his "Great Society" project, an ambitious program to promote racial equality, improve education, and fight poverty and other social issues.

Still, Johnson despised communism and believed in Eisenhower's domino theory—if South Vietnam fell, so would all of Southeast Asia. He was appalled by the idea of losing Vietnam to communism on his watch and wanted a decisive victory. His domestic and foreign goals, however, were politically at odds.

JOHNSON'S DILEMMA

When Johnson became president in late 1963, it was an ideal time for him to carry out the reforms he believed necessary to improve society. The Civil Rights Movement was gaining broader support, there was a Democratic majority in both houses of Congress, and Johnson had high approval ratings from the American public. The problem was that 1964 was a presidential election year. To properly launch his social programs, he would need to be reelected.

Johnson was campaigning as a moderate peace candidate, and he repeatedly assured Americans that he didn't want to "send American boys . . . to do what Asian boys ought to be doing for themselves."[1] Privately, however, he felt there was no question of the United States withdrawing from Vietnam. Doing so would almost certainly mean the country would fall to communism. This move would also damage the global credibility of the United States.

The situation in South Vietnam had worsened since Diem's assassination. One of Diem's generals took over the leadership of the country, only to be quickly ousted by another. Weary after nearly 20 years of war and turbulent leadership, South Vietnam's morale was low. The Vietcong took advantage of the political instability by becoming more aggressive. Johnson sent his secretary of defense, Robert McNamara (1916–2009), to visit Vietnam and decide on the best course of action.

STRATEGY FACT

Johnson worried that if he escalated the war before the election, he'd be in danger of losing the support of the public.

South Vietnam would bounce from leader to leader until Nguyen Van Thieu (1923–2001) became president in 1965. He remained in the role until 1975.

MCNAMARA'S PLAN

McNamara was determined to find a solution that was compatible with Johnson's Great Society goals and would keep the communists from overtaking South Vietnam. Eventually, McNamara became convinced that the United States should take direct military action against North Vietnam. He believed that a gradually escalating aerial bombing campaign of North Vietnam would pressure the communists to stop supporting the Vietcong and seek a diplomatic resolution. A slow escalation would be less likely to tempt the Soviet Union and China to enter the war directly.

Robert McNamara pointing to a map of Vietnam

credit: Marion S. Trikosko, *U.S. News & World Report*

When McNamara presented this idea to other presidential advisors, there was much doubt and dissent, especially among the top U.S. military advisors. Most believed that, because of the communists' determination, the only way to win in Vietnam would be to initiate a powerful offensive against North Vietnam right from the start, instead of slowly building up. They believed the ultimate goal shouldn't be negotiation, but the thorough destruction of the will and capabilities of North Vietnam. A slow escalation of action, they warned, would simply get American troops stuck in Vietnam for an indefinite period with little hope of success.

McNamara and other policymakers downplayed these serious concerns to President Johnson. Sometimes, they even blocked advisors from sharing their reservations with him.

Johnson accepted McNamara's plan. He believed the gradual escalation of the war would give him time to complete the election campaign without major military action, while allowing the South Vietnamese government time to stabilize. In April 1964, he quietly called upon military officials to develop a strategy of slowly increasing pressure and to begin choosing bombing targets in North Vietnam.

Meanwhile, Johnson continued to assure Americans that he sought peace.

McNamara's strategy had a legal problem, however. Striking North Vietnam was equivalent to an act of war, which, under the U.S. Constitution, required the consent of Congress. Johnson didn't want Congress to be distracted from domestic legislation by lengthy debates about the merits of the war. In August 1964, an event happened that allowed him to get around this problem.

WAR GAMES

In April 1964, about 35 to 45 members of the U.S. Joint Chiefs of Staff and Defense Department played a high-level war game to understand the potential consequences of an escalated bombing campaign of North Vietnam. The players each represented a specific nation or group in the conflict, behaving as they believed those parties would. The game's outcome revealed that no amount of bombing would make the North Vietnamese yield. The war would simply keep going. Similar games were played in September 1964 and 1965. These games not only reached the same conclusion, but indicated that eventually the U.S. public would rather withdraw from Vietnam than allow the war to keep escalating. These results had no effect on Johnson or other policymakers.

STRATEGY FACT

In 2007, declassified documents revealed that the second attack almost certainly did not occur. The misunderstanding was likely due to a misreading of intercepted communications, where reports about the first attack were accidentally read as a second, separate attack.

THE GULF OF TONKIN INCIDENT

On August 2, 1964, the USS *Maddox*, a Navy destroyer based in the Gulf of Tonkin, off the coast of North Vietnam, alerted the White House that three North Vietnamese torpedo boats had fired upon it. The *Maddox* returned fire. Aircraft from another U.S. destroyer joined in, damaging two of the North Vietnamese boats and disabling the third.

President Johnson decided not to retaliate. Although the attack had been called unprovoked, he was aware that South Vietnamese commandos, with U.S. Navy SEAL assistance, had been conducting covert strikes and raids against North Vietnamese port facilities. He assumed that the firing on the *Maddox* had been in retaliation for these covert operations.

Two days later, however, on August 4, President Johnson received word that the *Maddox* and another destroyer, the USS *Turner Joy*, had been fired upon by North Vietnam. This time, Johnson immediately called for retaliatory air strikes. What the U.S. public didn't know, though, was that even as Johnson ordered the strikes, naval authorities weren't sure that a second attack had actually occurred. The Johnson administration pressed forward with strikes anyway.

Johnson assured the American public that he didn't intend to expand the war, but he asked Congress to pass a resolution granting him broad power to act militarily against North Vietnam—just in case. Congress, alarmed by what seemed to be North Vietnam's intention to escalate the war, passed the Gulf of Tonkin Resolution on August 7. It gave the president power "to take all necessary measures" to repel an armed attack against U.S. forces and to prevent further aggression in Southeast Asia.

The USS *Maddox* in 1962

credit: PH1 Burwell, U.S. Navy

President Johnson now had unlimited power to escalate the war without having it officially declared. Johnson had also shown the American public that he could be both moderate and decisive when it came to war. He was elected by a landslide in November 1964.

AMERICA TAKES OVER

By the fall of 1964, the Vietcong were getting increasingly bold. On November 1, they staged a serious attack at Bien Hoa, a U.S. military airbase several miles north of Saigon. After slipping undetected into the surrounding countryside, they destroyed six B-57 bombers, damaged other aircraft, and left five Americans and two South Vietnamese dead. Then, they melted back into the countryside, unseen. Because the attack occurred just three days before the election, President Johnson didn't risk retaliation.

During December, the Vietcong made several large coordinated attacks throughout South Vietnam, including one in the heart of Saigon that killed two Americans. Despite pleading from frustrated military advisors and officials in Vietnam, President Johnson again did not respond.

A "HISTORIC MISTAKE"

Only two senators voted against the Gulf of Tonkin Resolution: Senator Wayne Morse (1900–1974) of Oregon and Senator Ernest Gruening (1887–1974) of Alaska. Senator Morse believed the resolution was a "historic mistake" because Congress was turning over its constitutional duty to declare war to the president. He also famously predicted that future generations would look upon it with dismay. You can read parts of the senators' official objections on this websites. Do you agree with any of their statements? Why do you think the Constitution gives Congress, not the president, the power to declare war? Do you think the Gulf of Tonkin Resolution was a mistake?

Congressional record senate 1964

OPERATION BARREL ROLL

Although President Johnson didn't publicly retaliate for the Vietcong attacks, he did approve ultra-secret air raid missions in Laos, a neutral country next to Vietnam. The United States bombed the part of the Ho Chi Minh Trail that was in Laos to prevent North Vietnam from using it to funnel troops and equipment to the South. Both the United States and North Vietnam kept the bombing secret because both countries were violating the Geneva Accords. North Vietnam was sending troops to the South and the United States was bombing a neutral country. The operation lasted from December 1964 until March 1973.

At last, when the Vietcong attacked the U.S. military base Camp Holloway in early February 1965, killing eight Americans and wounding 100, President Johnson reacted with force. Within hours, he authorized Operation Flaming Dart.

> U.S. aerial bombers and the South Vietnam air force blasted North Vietnamese military camps and communications centers.

Undeterred, the Vietcong attacked another U.S. base three days later, killing 20 Americans. Johnson ordered more raids, and bombs rained down on select targets in North Vietnam.

Moving from retaliatory strikes to escalating pressure, Johnson authorized Operation Rolling Thunder, the heavy bombing campaign of North Vietnam his administration had been planning for more than half a year. Starting on March 2, bombers struck military and industrial targets in North Vietnam for two months. But the bombing didn't cause significant damage to the North Vietnamese army, infrastructure, or supply route. Nor did it cause the communists to relent.

The biggest step toward escalation during this period was the introduction of ground troops in Vietnam. In February, General William Westmoreland (1914–2005), commander of the military forces in Vietnam, asked President Johnson to authorize two Marine combat battalions to protect U.S. air bases and South Vietnam's borders from communist infiltration.

Knowing this would deepen U.S. commitment to the war, many of Johnson's advisors objected. The U.S. ambassador to South Vietnam, General Maxwell Taylor (1901–1987), pointed out that a U.S. troop presence might remind the South Vietnamese of colonization and rouse dangerous patriotic feelings.

Undersecretary of State George Ball warned Johnson that once started, the United States would have to keep sending more and more troops until it would be unable to stop without "national humiliation." The Central Intelligence Agency, which had already warned the Johnson administration against deeper involvement in Vietnam, cautioned that even large numbers of U.S. ground troops would be unlikely to stop North Vietnam and the Vietcong.[2]

President Johnson was not persuaded by these objections. On March 8, 1965, 3,500 Marines splashed ashore at the port in Da Nang, Vietnam. They would be followed by another 80,000 within four months. At the end of 1965, there were almost 200,000 American troops fighting in Vietnam.

A WAR OF ATTRITION

Before the Marines landed in Vietnam, General Westmoreland had devised a three-phase strategy he believed would end the war. In Phase I, U.S. troops would halt the North Vietnam army's infiltration of the South by guarding military installations and potential infiltration points. In Phase II, American troops and allies would search and destroy guerrilla strongholds throughout South Vietnam. Phase III foresaw U.S. troops cleaning up any remaining enemy forces and handing control back to the South Vietnamese government.

STRATEGY FACT

Originally intended to last eight weeks, Operation Rolling Thunder ran nearly continuously for more than three years. During the operation, an average of 800 tons of bombs and missiles were dropped on North Vietnam every day.

Air Force F-105 Thunderchief pilots bomb a military target in 1966.

credit: U.S. Air Force

The Vietnam War had become an American war.

U.S. ALLIES

U.S. and South Vietnam troops did not fight alone. In response to President Johnson's request for help, a total of 400,000 troops from Australia, the Philippines, New Zealand, South Korea, and Thailand also fought in Vietnam. Why might these countries help the United States and South Vietnam?

Westmoreland's strategy was called a war of attrition. In such wars, the enemy is besieged with constant small attacks until it is too worn down to continue. Westmoreland believed that given the technologically advanced weaponry of the United States, plus its military training and vast financial resources, communist forces would eventually be overwhelmed. Optimistic, he estimated the completion of Phase III by the end of 1967.

Many of the U.S. combat troops who arrived in Vietnam in 1965 shared Westmoreland's optimism. Most were young enlisted soldiers, proud to fight on behalf of their country and eager to save another country from communism. Quite a few believed that the South Vietnamese would receive them as heroes. The reality of combat was a shock.

REALITY OF COMBAT

At first, morale among U.S. troops was high. In August 1965, only months after arriving, they scored a major victory in Operation Starlite. This offensive was triggered when a 17-year-old Vietcong defector warned the South Vietnam military leaders of an upcoming attack on the U.S. military base, Chu Lai. Instead, the Marines struck first, destroying a significant Vietcong stronghold and leaving 600 enemy dead. Months later, they scored another hard-fought victory at the Battle of Ia Drang.

Other successes would follow. But conventional battles such as these, where the United States could show its strengths, didn't happen every day. The Vietnam War was a different kind of war from what Americans had fought before. In Vietnam, soldiers spent much of their time waiting, watching, and looking for the enemy.

A U.S. Army soldier directs a helicopter to pick up the injured in South Vietnam, October 1966.

credit: U.S. Air Force

Unlike other wars that had a defined frontline where fighting occurred, in Vietnam, troops were constantly surrounded by danger. The Vietcong often launched guerrilla attacks by using booby traps, mines, and ambushes. As units patrolled infiltration points or potential Vietcong strongholds, they knew that at any moment, the wrong step on a booby-trapped path could trigger an explosion, or sniper fire might come blazing through the foliage. This created enormous mental stress.

Vietnam's sweltering climate didn't help. The sun's heat was brutal, especially for those soldiers—nicknamed "grunts"—who had to trudge through steaming jungles, tall elephant grass, or flooded rice paddies while wearing up to 80 pounds of equipment. Mosquitoes buzzed constantly, and leeches and ticks were persistent problems. During monsoon season, torrents of rain drenched the troops night and day. These conditions caused many soldiers to become sick with malaria, dysentery, and other diseases.

VIETNAM SLANG

Military slang was nothing new in the 1960s, but the jargon of Vietnam's soldiers was particularly unusual. Here are a few examples. Would you have guessed the meaning of any of these words?

Big Boys—tanks

Bird—aircraft, usually a helicopter

the Bush—any hostile jungle or field outside of basecamp

Frag—a fragmentation grenade

Hooch—a thatched hut or shack

Huey—a nickname for a Bell UH-1 Iroquois helicopter

In Country—Vietnam

Klick—1,000 kilometers

Kool-Aid—killed in action

River Rats—U.S. naval soldiers who manned patrol boats on Vietnam's waterways

Rock'n'Roll—firing a weapon on full automatic

Tea Party—radio code for an ambush

U.S. troops also realized that many South Vietnamese peasants didn't see them as heroes, especially after search-and-destroy missions became common. In these operations, troops acting on inside information would seek Vietcong in rural villages and hamlets. The troops would enter a village, evacuate the inhabitants to a secure location, arrest or kill any Vietcong, then destroy the village, usually by burning or bombing it.

Unsurprisingly, peasants deeply resented these missions. They hated being forced from their lands and made to witness the destruction of their homes. Worse, countless innocent civilians were killed at U.S. hands. A Vietcong soldier and a harmless peasant often looked the same, so troops never knew whether they faced a friend or foe. Nervous soldiers often killed anyone they remotely suspected of being a guerrilla, because they didn't want to put their entire team at risk. But these killings made many South Vietnamese unable to trust Americans any more than they could trust the Vietcong.

Soldiers lay down covering fire with a M60 machine gun, 1966.

credit: U.S. Army

DEFOLIATION AND PACIFICATION

Another major part of U.S. operations was a defoliation campaign called Operation Ranch Hand. The goal was to destroy farmland and crops that might be used by the Vietcong as a food source, and to strip South Vietnam's jungles and forests of the thick foliage that could conceal communist troop movement. From 1962 to 1971, the United States sprayed millions of gallons of herbicide on South Vietnam and those parts of Laos and Cambodia that sheltered the Ho Chi Minh Trail. By the time the operation ended, millions of acres of forests and 500,000 acres of farmland had been destroyed.

The United States also implemented pacification programs. These aimed to provide South Vietnamese villages with security and to "win the hearts and minds" of the people. For example, starting in August 1965, Marine rifle squads, medics, and members of the South Vietnamese army were sent to live in villages that were at risk of being targeted by the Vietcong. The Marines helped train the local militia, patrolled the area, and provided medical care and educational supplies.

AGENT ORANGE

Multiple herbicides were used to defoliate Vietnam, but the most effective was called Agent Orange. Agent Orange contained small amounts of a highly toxic chemical called dioxin that was later found to cause cancer, birth defects, tumors, Parkinson's disease, and other problems. Thousands of Vietnamese and U.S. veterans suffered serious health issues after being exposed to it. The United States stopped using Agent Orange in 1971, after it became well-known that it was unsafe for humans.

STALEMATE

By 1967, it was becoming clear that General Westmoreland's war of attrition wasn't going as well as expected. On the upside, the United States had won several large-scale battles and had kept the North Vietnam army from holding certain critical areas. In addition, communist forces consistently had a much higher body count than U.S. forces. This indicated to Westmoreland that it was only a matter of time before North Vietnam's forces would be too depleted to continue fighting.

TUNNEL RATS

American and allied troops known as tunnel rats were trained to engage in special search-and-destroy missions in Cu Chi tunnels. A soldier would slip into the tunnels to smoke out the enemy, gather intelligence, and ultimately demolish the tunnel with detonated charges. As the tunnels were often booby-trapped, being a tunnel rat was a highly dangerous job. Now, the tunnels serve as tourist attractions. You can see a video tour of one of the tunnels at this website. What might it have been like to descend into those tunnels during wartime?

 PS

🔍 Cu Chi tunnel video

But Westmoreland underestimated both the number of human resources the communists had and their determination to succeed. Even after suffering shockingly high casualties, the North Vietnam army and the Vietcong were able to rebuild their forces and launch ambushes with surprising quickness. Hundreds of thousands of North Vietnamese, and some South Vietnamese, were eager to fight for what they saw as the liberation of their country from foreign influence.

> Time and time again, U.S. troops would search and destroy a particular area, only for the Vietcong to eventually return in full force.

Other aspects of the campaign were equally frustrating. Both General Westmoreland and Secretary McNamara secretly admitted that Operation Rolling Thunder wasn't achieving its objectives. The bombing of North Vietnam hadn't slowed the resolve of the communist leadership nor prevented communist troops and equipment from reaching the South. In fact, despite the relentless bombing of the Ho Chi Minh Trail, the flow of troops and supplies on the trail actually increased after the bombing began in 1965.

The communists knew to play to their strengths. When they discovered their weakness in conventional combat, they relied more on guerrilla tactics. After being pounded by U.S. air power during battle, they learned to "cling to the belts" of Americans.[3] They knew that the United States wouldn't risk dropping bombs on American troops, so they stayed very close to Americans during fights.

The communists also used an extensive network of hand-dug tunnels built during the Indochina War. The Cu Chi tunnels ran from the Cu Chi district of Saigon to the Cambodian border, a distance of about 155 miles. The tunnels served different purposes, such as transporting troops and supplies, hiding from U.S. bombing raids or patrol sweeps, and mounting surprise attacks. Astonishingly elaborate, the tunnels included hospitals, sleeping quarters, kitchens, and even theaters.

Faced with such a determined enemy, U.S. troops began to grow demoralized. Although they continued to fight bravely, many turned to drugs, such as marijuana and heroin, for comfort. Many counted down the days until their one-year tour of duty was over.

Even so, General Westmoreland and the military brass remained convinced that another large infusion of troops would enable the United States to beat the communists. But others—especially the American public—were beginning to doubt of the plan. We'll learn about how the United States reacted to the war in the next chapter.

KEY QUESTIONS

- **Why did President Johnson's political goals have such a large impact on his decision to go to war in Vietnam?**
- **If the Gulf of Tonkin Resolution hadn't passed, and Congress had to declare war to escalate the conflict, might the war might have played out differently? Why?**
- **How was guerrilla warfare different from traditional warfare?**

VOCAB LAB

Write down what you think each word means. What root words can you find to help you? What does the context of the word tell you?

attrition, **casualty**, **covert**, **credibility**, **defector**, **defoliation**, **dissent**, **domino theory**, **escalate**, **herbicide**, **moral**, **sniper fire**, **pacification**, **stronghold**, and **troops**.

Compare your definitions with those of your friends or classmates. Did you all come up with the same meanings? Turn to the text and glossary if you need help.

DEAR HOME

The Vietnam War was a terrifying, life-changing experience for the soldiers who fought there. The estimated average age of a soldier was 22 years old, and 61 percent of those who died were under 21. Many soldiers in Vietnam wrote to their families as often as possible and loved receiving letters in return. Being able to write home and receive letters helped them stay connected to the outside world and document their experiences.

---

* **Read some letters and excerpts of letters written by soldiers in Vietnam.**

 letter excerpts Donn

 last letter from Vietnam

 letters Paul commentary

 PRI 43 years later

* **After you read or listen to them, consider the following questions.**

  * What were the reasons some of these men went to Vietnam?

  * What are some of the different tones and emotions expressed in the letters?

  * What surprises you about the letters?

  * How did the letter writers' experiences differ? How were they similar?

* **Imagine that you are a combat soldier in Vietnam.** Write a letter or email home discussing your experiences. What would you want to talk about? What would you want to know about back home?

To investigate more, imagine that you are a South Vietnamese peasant during the war who was evacuated because of the Vietcong threat. Write a letter to a relative outside of Vietnam describing what wartime life is like. How do you feel about the Vietcong? How might you feel about the United States? What are your fears?

Chapter 4

Resistance and Division

How did opposition to the Vietnam War divide the United States?

IN 1965, PROFESSORS AT THE UNIVERSITY OF MICHIGAN ORGANIZED A TEACH-IN.

WE ARE ENCOURAGED BY HOW MANY STUDENTS ARE HERE AND WOULD LIKE THIS TO BE AN OPEN FORUM.

AMERICA WAS DIVIDED BETWEEN THOSE WHO WANTED PEACE, KNOWN AS *DOVES*...

STOP THE WAR!

...AND THE HAWKS, WHO SUPPORTED THE WAR AND THOUGHT THE U.S. NEEDED TO ESCALATE THE EFFORT.

GO ARMY!

The escalation of the Vietnam War triggered the most powerful antiwar movement in U.S. history and caused a fierce divide in the country.

As the war heated up in 1965, the American public slowly realized how deeply the United States was involved. Until then, President Johnson had successfully presented himself as a leader of moderation and peace. But as the United States sank further into the conflict, he no longer seemed like a peacekeeper. Opposition to his policies grew and the United States descended into an ugly war of its own at home.

Until the Gulf of Tonkin incident, few Americans paid much attention to the war, and those who did supported Johnson. Rumblings of discontent began in late 1964, but they grew louder after Johnson's retaliatory bombing of North Vietnam in February 1965.

Inspired by the success of the protests of the Civil Rights Movement, peace activists began to stage antiwar demonstrations. These activists had fought for nuclear disarmament during the 1950s, and were joined by many intellectuals from American universities.

SEEDS OF DISSENT

In March 1965, the University of Michigan held a teach-in to bring attention to the Vietnam conflict. More than 3,000 students, teachers, and guest speakers attended the teach-in. Columbia University promptly followed, and within a few months, more than 100 universities had held teach-ins. Pro-war supporters saw the teach-ins as forms of protest and often picketed the events.

President Johnson was worried by the amount of attention the teach-ins were generating. By now, his Great Society plans were well underway. The previous year, he had brought about the passage of the Civil Rights Act of 1964 and now he was in the middle of developing the Voting Rights Act. He didn't want any criticism about the war to distract the public or his political colleagues from his domestic plans.

To reassure the public, he delivered an uplifting, nationally televised speech at Johns Hopkins University on April 7, 1965. He emphasized America's promise to support South Vietnam in its struggle, restated his commitment to peace, and described a $1 billion offer to North Vietnam to improve its economy in exchange for ending the war.

The public was mostly relieved by his words, and support for his policies remained high. But the antiwar movement had already gained momentum. The next day, a massive protest took place in New York City. About 20,000 people participated, including folksingers Judy Collins, Joan Baez, and Phil Ochs. Their antiwar songs would become representative of the times.

Johnson made two key speeches about Vietnam in the first half of 1965. You can read the text of these speeches at these websites. How do the speeches differ in tone? What statements might people have found persuasive or reassuring in each speech?

 President Johnson April 7

 President Johnson July 28

HAWKS AND DOVES

Despite President Johnson's desire to manage the war with "as low a level of public noise as possible,"[1] the war came into ever-sharpening focus in American lives. Throughout 1965 and early 1966, several large antiwar protests took place across the country, but these demonstrations made no dent in overall support for the conflict. The majority of the country stood firmly behind Johnson.

The different viewpoints gradually divided the country into what became known as hawks and doves. Hawks supported escalation of the war, while doves wanted the war slowed down. As antiwar protests grew more frequent, hawks began to form their own counter-protests and rallies.

Most hawks backed the war because they despised communism, believed in the domino theory, and thought U.S. national security was at stake. Others simply believed that all Americans should support the government and military during wartime, no matter what. These citizens were outraged by antiwar protests because they showed a divided America to the enemy.

Dove objections to the war were more varied. Some doves were pacifists who objected to American involvement in Vietnam because they opposed all wars. Others, often called liberals, weren't necessarily against all wars, but believed this particular war was wrong. They argued that Vietnam had a right to choose what kind of country it would be. The United States had no right to interfere, even if Vietnam chose a communist-led government. Still others believed the United States might be entitled to interfere if its national interest was at stake, but the threat of communism taking over Southeast Asia wasn't a good enough reason.

The terms "hawk" and "dove" were first used to describe pro-war and antiwar supporters during the War of 1812. The terms were revived by a spring 1966 Gallup poll that asked Americans which they considered themselves to be. You can examine the results of that poll and later polls that asked the same question. How did opinions change with the passing of time? What don't these results tell us about the public's opinion on the war?

 Gallup hawks doves Vietnam

Some activists protested the military's use of chemical weapons, such as Agent Orange and napalm. Napalm was a deadly acid-gasoline substance the military used in flamethrowers and incendiary bombs. Far more destructive than ordinary fire, napalm actually melted flesh and caused deep wounds that were difficult to heal. Thousands of civilians in Vietnam died from napalm injuries. Protestors picketed the Dow Chemical Co., which produced napalm for the government.

A small minority of protesters actually supported the Vietnamese communists. Their inclusion in protests frequently caused disputes between various antiwar groups that worried that communist associations would make the government and pro-war advocates immediately disregard their viewpoints. And indeed, some hawks automatically branded all antiwar protesters as communists, regardless of their views.

STRATEGY FACT

In November 1965, Norman Morrison, a young pacifist, Quaker, and father of three, set himself on fire within view of Robert McNamara's window at the Pentagon to protest the war. During the course of the war, eight Americans self-immolated in protest.

Anti-war protesters in Wichita, Kansas, 1967

credit: U.S. National Archives and Records Administration

THE DRAFT

Of all the antiwar protesters of the era, those who opposed the draft are probably most remembered. The draft, formally known as conscription, is the process of selecting American men between the ages of 18 and 25 to serve in the armed forces when the government finds it necessary. All men had to register with the Selective Service System within 30 days of their eighteenth birthday—they received a draft card as proof of registration.

In July 1965, President Johnson announced that he was increasing the draft numbers from 17,000 to 35,000 per month. This prompted a cry of outrage that lasted almost the entire duration of the war.

Many young men were strongly opposed to fighting in a war they considered immoral. A wave of protests took place on college campuses throughout the country, and numerous organizations were formed to resist the draft. Although it was a criminal offense, thousands of youths publicly burned, mutilated, or turned in their draft cards during the next few years. It couldn't stop them from being drafted, but it was a powerful symbolic act.

People also objected to the inequities that arose from the draft. A disproportionate percentage of young men sent to Vietnam by the draft—a staggering 80 percent—were from poor and working-class families. This was partly because local draft boards, which decided who would go or stay, were usually composed of local community members. Families with connections to draft board members could sometimes convince them to give their son a deferment, which meant he wouldn't have to serve. Children of families without political contacts, usually those who were poor or working class, were more likely to be drafted.

THE DRAFT LOTTERY

To fix the draft's unfairness, in 1969, the government instituted a draft lottery based on birth dates. A slip of paper for each day of the year, including February 29, was put into 366 plastic capsules. One capsule was randomly selected from a glass jar. The birth date in the first capsule selected was assigned the number 001, which meant that men with that birthdate would be required to report to a Selective Service office to be assessed. The drawing process continued until every day of the year had an assigned number. The lower your number, the more likely you were to be drafted. What do you think it was like for men who had a lower number?

This imbalance was further increased by a law that allowed young men enrolled in college to defer military service until after graduation. Most poor and working-class families, particularly African Americans, couldn't afford college. This meant they were more likely to be sent to Vietnam. Do you think this was fair? Why or why not?

> Hundreds of thousands of young men actively protested the draft, but just as many quietly tried to avoid it.

It was common for draftees to exaggerate or even invent a medical condition that would exclude them from serving. There were also doctors willing to confirm these imaginary illnesses. Some took illegal drugs that made them appear unhealthy at their draft board physical exam. Others pretended to be gay—homosexuals couldn't serve in the armed forces.

Thousands of people illegally avoided the draft by leaving the country. Between 1965 and 1973, about 100,000 to 150,000 American war resisters went to live in Canada or other countries to evade the draft. Educated young men with financially secure families were most likely to take advantage of this option.

About 170,000 men avoided serving in the war due to their status as conscientious objectors (COs). A CO is someone who refuses to serve in a war or bear arms based on religious or moral grounds. If you belonged to a religious group known for opposing all war, such as Quakers or Mennonites, you were most likely to get approved. If you opposed the war for political reasons, approval was less likely. About 300,000 men applied for CO status and were rejected.

A draft card from 1972

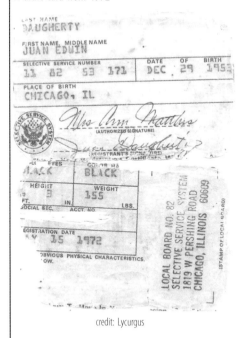

credit: Lycurgus

The men who avoided the draft were scornfully labelled draft dodgers by war supporters. They were often looked down upon in their communities and sometimes even within their own families. The older generation, many of whom had fought in World War II, couldn't understand why young men didn't feel obligated to serve their country. How might a young man have responded to this criticism?

HELLO, HIPPIES!

The mid-1960s saw a deeply divided American society as multiple movements for social change swept across the land. Voices that had been historically disregarded or suppressed were now making themselves heard. Young people, sick of both the government and American society, shrugged off traditional roles and values. Some not only opposed the war and resisted the draft, but also chose a new, free-living, no-rules lifestyle incomprehensible to older folks. These were the legendary hippies.

For hippies, life was about peace, love, and self-indulgence. Mainly coming from white, middle class homes, many went to live on communes, where they grew their own crops and shared everything, from chores to food. Drug use was a central part of the hippie lifestyle, as was nudity and open sexuality. Further infuriating the clean-cut older generation, many hippies, both men and women, had long hair and wore bright, flowing clothes with unusual patterns.

Hippies weren't leaders of the antiwar movement, but they were often part of marches and protests. They carried banners and signs with the now iconic slogan "Make Love, Not War." The flower was their symbol of passive resistance, and they sometimes offered flowers to policemen or soldiers at protests or even placed flowers in the barrels of pointed guns.

David Miller, 22, was the first person to be prosecuted for burning his draft card. He served two years in prison for the crime. You can see his picture and read an article about his life at this website.

 David Miller draft

Antiwar protesters face off with police.

credit: U.S. Department of Defense

Although hippies might not have swayed public opinion much, their colorful presence did direct more attention to the war. Hippies and hippie culture highlighted the sharp polarization of the nation.

AFRICAN AMERICANS AND VIETNAM

As many white young adults found identity and meaning in the hippie movement, many black young adults found similar fulfillment in the Black Power Movement. This movement promoted the philosophy that blacks shouldn't merely aim to integrate with whites, but should embrace their own power and identity as black people.

Black people who embraced this movement began to focus more on economic betterment and encouraged each other to take pride in their heritage. Adopting the slogan "Black is Beautiful," they began referring to themselves as black instead of Negro, and wore their hair in natural styles.

> Some wore African clothing and changed their names to emphasize their heritage.

Shaking off fears of jeopardizing President Johnson's Great Society plans, black leaders and civil rights groups began to speak out in opposition to the Vietnam War. Black nationalist leader Malcolm X (1925–1965) was one of the first black leaders to speak out against the war, denouncing it even before Johnson sent the Marines in. Other leaders pointed out the draft discrepancies and noted that the death rate of black soldiers was disproportionately high.

MUHAMMAD ALI

Muhammad Ali, the legendary heavyweight boxer, was a famous conscientious objector. Ali claimed CO status because his Muslim religion didn't permit killing. He refused to be inducted into the army and insisted he'd rather go to jail. He was convicted of refusing to report for induction and was stripped of his heavyweight title. In 1971, his conviction was overturned by the U.S. Supreme Court. Watch him argue against going to war at this website. How does Ali shut down those who objected to his refusal to report? Do you agree?

 Muhammad Ali street heat

Martin Luther King Jr. and Malcolm X at a rare meeting in 1964. Both fought for the rights of African Americans, though with different goals and different methods. Both were assassinated in the 1960s.

credit: Marion S. Trikosko

Many blacks scoffed at the idea that the United States had noble intentions in wanting to establish a democratic system of free and fair elections in Vietnam—when the government regularly denied these rights to black Americans. And in 1967, Dr. Martin Luther King Jr. (1929–1968) famously called for the "madness" of the war to cease. He argued that the war increased the suffering of Vietnam's poor and of poor Americans, because the war diverted funds from the Great Society programs.

Like the hippies, blacks contributed to the protest against the war, but did little to sway mainstream society.

TURNING OF THE TIDE

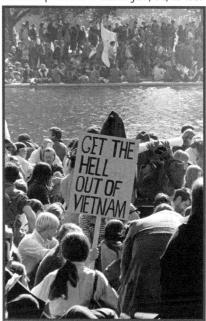

Vietnam protesters in Washington, DC, in 1967

credit: Frank Wolfe

What did finally nudge general public opinion toward disapproval of the war? A tangle of overlapping factors. For one thing, Americans started to become tired of the war. Most polls in 1966 and 1967 showed President Johnson's handling of the war was generally still supported by a majority, but in some polls, the majority disapproved.

The president tried to calm anxieties by reassuring the public that the United States was winning and wearing down the Vietcong. As evidence, General Westmoreland provided weekly body counts of dead Vietcong. These figures did little to appease the public, however. In 1966, 6,100 U.S. soldiers died in the war and in 1967, another 11,153 were killed. No matter how many thousands more Vietcong died, the steadily rising number of American deaths was becoming intolerable for the public.

Another factor was the pervasiveness of war news on television. In the 1960s, television had only just become a standard feature in American homes. Unlike during previous wars, Americans could watch the realities of war unfold with their own eyes, in their own living rooms, leading many to call it a television war. Although violent scenes weren't frequently shown, the war's constant presence might have magnified the public's feelings of weariness and uncertainty.

A third factor—and one of the most controversial—was press coverage of the war. At the war's peak in 1968, more than 600 accredited international journalists were on the ground in Vietnam. Most journalists were based in Saigon and received their news from military officials, but many others accompanied combat troops into action.

Vietnam was the first twentieth-century U.S. war without government censorship of media coverage. In World Wars I and II, all media reports were filtered through the Office of War Information before being shown to the public. The Vietnam War had no such limits.

One well-known example of negative reporting was Morley Safer's (1931–2016) film report in 1965. It showed U.S. Marines on a search-and-destroy mission setting fire to the thatched huts of the village of Cam Ne, while anguished Vietnamese peasants looked on. Although this report was shocking, it was unusual at that time. You can watch parts of the report at this website. How does this compare to news that is shown on television today?

WARNING: Footage at this website might be disturbing for some viewers.

Morley Safer
Cam Ne

Some argue that the media turned the public against the war with too many negative reports. However, researcher Daniel Hallin's analyses of Vietnam War media coverage show that until early 1968, reporting on the war was largely positive.[3] Many pre-1968 reports were straightforward battlefield recaps and personal accounts of American boys in action to show folks back home what they were doing. Only 22 percent of pre-1968 news reports were combat footage, and these rarely showed dead or badly wounded soldiers.

However, some journalists presented stories that were critical of the war, or showed a reality different from the one U.S. officials were presenting. Such reports cast the United States in a bad light, and may have negatively affected public opinion, but they were uncommon before 1968.

Media reports took a noticeably more negative turn in early 1968, but public disapproval of the war had already grown considerably by that point. Plus, a fourth factor occurred that helped shift public opinion—the actions of the U.S. government itself.

THE TET OFFENSIVE

By late 1967, President Johnson was under immense pressure. With nearly half a million U.S. troops in Vietnam, the military was pushing for still more to be sent over. Antiwar protests were swelling. Johnson's approval ratings were dropping, and more politicians were turning against the war.

Even Johnson's loyal Defense Secretary McNamara could no longer support the war. He saw the conflict as futile and advised Johnson to start scaling back. When this advice was rejected, McNamara resigned.

U.S. Marines during the Tet Offensive

credit: Schulimson

Hoping to boost public morale, Johnson decided to feed the public encouraging news about the war. In mid-November 1967, he flew General Westmoreland back from Vietnam. With more optimism than honesty, he reassured both the U.S. Senate and public that the Vietcong ranks were thinning rapidly and that the war's end was in sight.

> But these assurances were quickly thrown into doubt.

The eve of the Vietnamese Lunar New Year, called Tet, dawned on January 30, 1968. That day, nearly 70,000 North Vietnam and Vietcong forces launched more than 100 simultaneous attacks in cities and towns throughout South Vietnam. They were able to breach many places the United States had thought secure, including the U.S. embassy and South Vietnam's presidential palace.

The United States and South Vietnam were stunned. They hadn't believed the communists were powerful enough for such an offensive. Rallying quickly, the two military forces fiercely battled the communists for the next two months in a move called the Tet Offensive. By the end of March, nearly 37,000 communist troops lay dead. The United States suffered 2,500 losses.

The Tet Offensive was a military victory for the United States, but the magnitude and force of the attack was a huge blow to the American public's morale. The government had only recently assured the public that the Vietcong were weakening. If that was true, how could they have taken the military by surprise and caused thousands of American deaths? This gap between official statements and actual events made more people mistrust the government. The majority of Americans now thought it had been a mistake to enter the war.

President Johnson and the military blamed the media for the low national morale. The media followed the Tet Offensive battles carefully, and television viewers saw more explicit scenes of violence and destruction than they had before. Journalists' questions and comments also developed a more skeptical tone. While this might have played a factor in poor morale, so did the rising U.S. death toll and the unlikelihood that the war was near a conclusion.

The Tet Offensive was a crushing military defeat for the communists, but the knowledge that U.S. public opinion had turned against the war was a great psychological victory for the Vietcong. They used this knowledge to motivate their troops and to keep pressure on the United States.

JOHNSON DECLINES TO RUN

In March 1968, General Westmoreland was still pushing for a large troop increase. After weeks of discussions with his advisors, President Johnson decided against it. In a television address on March 31, he instead called for limiting U.S. bombing strikes on North Vietnam. Then, he shocked the nation by announcing that he wouldn't seek reelection.

Johnson also opened the door to negotiations with North Vietnam. Envoys from both countries met in Paris, France, to discuss ways of ending the war. Both the United States and North Vietnam were eager to resolve the conflict, but talks failed as neither nation would yield on the political future of South Vietnam. The United States wouldn't agree to any communists in the government and North Vietnam wouldn't agree to the absence of communists.

Running on a campaign of promising to end the war, Republican Richard Nixon (1913–1994) would become the next president. In the next chapter, we'll see how President Nixon withdrew the United States from the conflict, but further divided America.

VOCAB LAB

Write down what you think each word means. What root words can you find to help you? What does the context of the word tell you?

activist, **censorship**, **conscientious objector**, **deferment**, **draft**, **Great Society**, **hippies**, **incendiary**, **integrate**, **intellectual**, **polarization**, **protest**, and **teach-in**.

Compare your definitions with those of your friends or classmates. Did you all come up with the same meanings? Turn to the text and glossary if you need help.

KEY QUESTIONS

- What responsibility do you think the media have during wartime? Has this responsibility changed since the Vietnam War?

- Have you ever participated in a political protest or demonstration? Did it make a difference?

- What do you think today's wars might be like if the United States started up the draft again?

MUSIC OF THE VIETNAM ERA

As the Vietnam War escalated, folksingers began expressing their condemnation of the war through music. These songs expressed the emotions and frustrations that many were feeling, and promoted a sense of unity in a highly divisive time. Singers such as Bob Dylan (1941–), Phil Ochs (1940–1976), Joan Baez (1941–), Arlo Guthrie (1947–), and Barry McGuire (1935–) were among the leading artists of the era. They became legends for their Vietnam era music and lyrics.

- **Search for Vietnam protest songs and listen to examples of anti-war music from this time.** Consider the following questions.

  - What are some of the different messages the songs tried to convey?

  - What different emotions did each song appeal to?

  - In what ways might these songs have influenced youth behavior?

  - Can you name any modern songs that relate to today's political or social issues? What topics do they cover?

- **Write your own song or poem that expresses feelings and opinions about a current political or social concern.**

  - What point of view will you write from?

  - What images will you use to get your point across?

  - How will you use rhythm to convey meaning or emotion?

To investigate more, imagine that you live during the Vietnam era and want to show your support for the war. Create a slogan to put on a placard or banner. Who would be your intended audience? What message would you want to deliver? If you were against the war, what would you come up with?

Chapter 5 ▶
Spiraling to the End

How did the Vietnam War end for the United States?

IN 1968, RICHARD NIXON WON THE PRESIDENCY ON A PLATFORM OF ENDING THE VIETNAM WAR.

LIKE JOHNSON FOUR YEARS BEFORE, NIXON FOUND THAT ENDING THE WAR WITHOUT FAILING WAS IMPOSSIBLE. HE SLOWLY WITHDREW U.S. TROOPS.

BUT FAILURE WAS INEVITABLE.

U.S. officials managed to come to an agreement with North Vietnam that set the stage for U.S. withdrawal of troops. The withdrawal left South Vietnam with few resources with which to defend itself.

When Richard Nixon won the presidential election of 1968, the United States had just experienced a devastating year. Civil rights heroes Martin Luther King Jr. and Robert Kennedy (1925–1968) had been assassinated. These events deepened the public's cynicism. Antiwar protests outside the Democratic National Convention in Chicago had turned into a violent battle between protesters and law enforcement. And more than 16,500 U.S. soldiers had died in Vietnam.

President Nixon had an enormous task ahead of him. By now, most Americans wanted the war to end quickly, but they were divided about how it should happen. Many hawks wanted to take a tougher stance against North Vietnam, even if it meant bombing them into submission. Doves wanted an immediate withdrawal of troops.

Neither plan was possible for political reasons.

President Nixon was a hawk and a fervent anti-communist. He would have considered increasing aggression against North Vietnam to force it to yield, but knew this would cause a domestic uproar. He couldn't call for an immediate withdrawal of troops either, as it would damage U.S. credibility and leave South Vietnam vulnerable.

NIXON'S PLAN FOR PEACE

Nixon's idea was to gradually withdraw U.S. troops and pass all military responsibilities back to South Vietnam. As the withdrawal occurred, a small number of U.S. military advisors would train the South Vietnamese military, as at the beginning of the war. This plan was known as Vietnamization.

In June 1969, Nixon starting putting his plan into action. He announced the withdrawal of 25,000 U.S. troops from Vietnam by the end of August and another 40,000 within three months. In September, he announced that he'd withdraw another 35,000 soldiers and reduce the draft call. The public was delighted.

Nixon also continued the Paris peace talks that President Johnson had initiated. But two major points of disagreement stalled the discussion—the withdrawal of troops and the political structure of South Vietnam.

The United States wanted American and North Vietnamese troops to simultaneously withdraw from South Vietnam, and wanted South Vietnam's President Nguyen Thieu to remain in power. North Vietnam was firmly against withdrawing their troops and were insistent that President Thieu step down. They wanted a coalition government with Vietcong representatives.

Nixon saw his job as achieving "peace with honor." He needed to get the United States out of the war without being perceived as having abandoned South Vietnam.

Nixon was frustrated by North Vietnam's stubbornness, but the communist country wouldn't budge. North Vietnam was under no particular time pressure to end the war—and they knew that Nixon was.

THE MADMAN THEORY

Aware of the United States' disadvantage in the negotiating process, Nixon sought to pressure North Vietnam by using what he called the madman theory. He believed he could frighten North Vietnam into being more flexible in negotiations if he acted like he was willing to use nuclear force.

In playing this out, Nixon made multiple moves. First, he began bombing Cambodia without telling the U.S. public. In February 1969, just weeks after his inauguration, American military advisors in Vietnam informed Nixon that about 40,000 communist troops had set up bases in Cambodia, and that bombing would help break them up. Nixon agreed, believing that the bombings would both weaken the communists and further his madman image.

Bombing Cambodia

credit: U.S. Air Force

> On March 19, the carpet bombing
> of Cambodia began.

Nixon also tried to convince the Soviet Union that he was uncontrollable in the hopes that the Soviets would pressure Hanoi into changing its position. In March 1969, Nixon's national security advisor, Henry Kissinger (1923–), hinted to the Soviet ambassador to the United States that Nixon would use excessive force if North Vietnam didn't bend. The Soviets didn't react, however, and nothing changed.

On July 15, Nixon sent a personal letter to Ho Chi Minh through a French envoy that asked to move forward with a peaceable resolution. But he also instructed the envoy to deliver a verbal message that the United States would resort to "measures of great consequence and force"[1] if an agreement wasn't reached by November 1. Nixon received a bland reply from Hanoi on August 30. It stated that peace would come if the United States withdrew its troops and allowed the people of Vietnam to sort out their own matters.

Nixon even went so far as to call for a secret, world-wide nuclear alert in late October 1969. Unknown to the American public, he sent B-52 bombers with nuclear warheads racing toward the border of the Soviet Union. He wanted to show the Soviets how crazy he was, and to pressure them into leaning on Hanoi.

The Soviets did appear to think Nixon unbalanced, but the tactic didn't make them stop supporting North Vietnam. And Hanoi did not bow to pressure. The November 1 deadline passed without incident. Do you think President Nixon made a good choice in pretending to be a madman? Even if the ploy had worked, what might some of the repercussions of that strategy have been?

OPERATION MENU

The bombing of Cambodia, Operation Menu, was top secret. Cambodia was a neutral country under the Geneva Accords, and aggressions on its soil violated the agreement. Nixon also wanted to keep the operation quiet because he knew that bombing another country wouldn't mesh with his statements that he was ending the war. So Nixon told neither Congress nor the American public. Documents were even falsified to indicate that pilots were bombing South Vietnam instead of Cambodia. The bombings continued for more than three years, only ending in 1972 when Congress learned of the operation.

NIXON AND ANTIWAR PROTESTS

Read the text of President Nixon's November 3, 1969, speech at the American Presidency Project website. Which aspects of Nixon's speech do you think were most convincing? Least convincing? If you were to write a letter for or against the speech, what arguments would you use?

 Nixon speech silent majority

By fall 1969, antiwar protesters were getting impatient. Wanting to keep pressure on the government, they organized moratoriums, or large antiwar demonstrations, in cities across the country. The first moratorium took place on October 15, 1969. Hundreds of thousands of people protested in Boston, New York, Washington, and other places.

While Nixon wanted to seem like a madman to the communists, he wanted to appear reasonable and strong at home. On November 3, in a nationally televised address, he explained his policy of Vietnamization and the various steps he had taken to secure peace. He even pointed to the letters between himself and Ho Chi Minh as proof of his reasonableness and North Vietnam's stubbornness. He concluded by asking the "silent majority" of Americans to unite and support his policies.[2]

The public reaction to the speech was very positive. In the days that followed, the White House received tens of thousands of calls, letters, and telegrams of support. Then, days after Nixon's speech, the public learned of a horrific atrocity that had occurred in Vietnam.

The atrocity is known as
the My Lai Massacre.

My Lai was a South Vietnamese village believed to be housing Vietcong. A military unit was ordered to conduct a search-and-destroy mission of My Lai and to assume that everyone in the village was Vietcong or a sympathizer. When the soldiers entered the village, they found mostly women, children, and old men. Even so, they brutally killed everyone. The event took place in March 1968, but the military covered it up until a soldier helped expose the event.

News of this atrocity sparked international outrage, but the American public was particularly appalled. On November 15, the largest antiwar moratorium yet occurred. Approximately 500,000 people marched in Washington, DC. Some 40,000 of these marched silently toward the Capitol wearing placards bearing the names of dead U.S. soldiers or destroyed Vietnamese villages.

Nixon didn't publicly acknowledge the protests. He didn't believe policy should be made "in the streets" by those with the "loudest voices."[3] He was also angry with protesters because he believed his policy was the right approach to ending the war. He didn't seem to understand that protesters no longer trusted the government to do the right thing. Several months later, he made another decision that heightened this mistrust.

KENT STATE SHOOTINGS

On April 20, 1970, President Nixon gave the nation an update on the war in Vietnam. He said South Vietnam was assuming its military responsibilities well, and that he would withdraw another 150,000 troops within a year. He expressed confidence that peace was finally in sight. But confusingly, 10 days later, he announced he was sending ground troops, along with South Vietnamese troops, to fight in Cambodia for a limited period to rout North Vietnamese communists.

> There was immediate uproar following this announcement.

Enraged students renewed their protests. How could Nixon be winding down the war if he was sending troops to fight in another country?

People in My Lai, just before being killed

credit: Ronald L. Haeberle

On May 4, days after Nixon's speech, about 500 students at Kent State University gathered for an unauthorized protest at a campus rally. The Ohio National Guard, which was there to keep order, fired tear gas at them to make them disband. The demonstrators heckled the guardsmen and threw the teargas canisters back at them, along with rocks.

In the chaos, the guardsmen fired a volley of shots, killing four students and injuring nine.

The deaths triggered a wave of furious protests across the country. Some 400 colleges and universities shut down, as horrified students and professors went on strike. Nixon's attitude created further outrage. He didn't extend his sympathy to the dead students' families, and appeared to blame the protesters. Many people thought that Nixon should have condemned the guardsmen for shooting unarmed students.

Students weren't the only ones appalled by Nixon's Cambodia invasion. Many politicians, both Democrats and Republicans, felt that the President had overstepped his boundaries. Republican Senator John Cooper (1901–1991) and Democratic Senator Frank Church (1924–1984) cosponsored a bill to eliminate funding for the Cambodian invasion. A modified version of the Cooper-Church Amendment was passed by both houses of Congress on January 5, 1971.

To limit presidential power, on June 24, 1970, the Senate also voted to repeal the Gulf of Tonkin Resolution. President Nixon was angered by these acts. He felt that they weakened the U.S. position in the ongoing Paris peace talks and gave a psychological victory to North Vietnam.

The public's reaction to the Cooper-Church amendment was mixed. Read some letters supporting and condemning the amendment. Which arguments do you find most compelling? Why?

letter against Cooper-Church

letter supporting Cooper-Church

BACK IN VIETNAM

As the domestic conflict raged in the United States, soldiers were still fighting in Vietnam. Military officials were infuriated by Nixon's decision to withdraw troops. They argued that the Vietcong had been seriously weakened in the Tet Offensive, and that the United States should take advantage of it. Further, after General Creighton Abrams (1914–1974) replaced General Westmoreland in 1968, the military felt they were getting better results.

General Abrams had abandoned the war of attrition and instead strongly focused on pacification programs. This included a "clear and hold" strategy. Soldiers would clear a village of Vietcong, and then, instead of destroying the village, would protect it against further Vietcong encroachment. Why might this method work better?

Progress was also being made in weakening the Vietcong infrastructure through a program called Operation Phoenix. In this highly controversial program, the CIA, U.S. military, and South Vietnam officials shared information on the Vietcong and enlisted villagers' help in finding and then executing, capturing, or converting them. About 60,000 Vietcong were neutralized under this operation—along with countless innocent villagers. Nevertheless, the program did loosen the Vietcong's hold on South Vietnam.

Despite the military's insistence that the situation was improving, Vietnamization continued. In February 1971, the United States gave the South Vietnamese army primary responsibility for a mission called Operation Lam Son 719. The goal was to destroy part of the Ho Chi Minh Trail supply route in Laos. The U.S. military would provide only logistical, air, and artillery support from the South Vietnamese border.

FRAGGING

Military officials may have been satisfied by the war's progress at this point, but morale among soldiers was extremely low. They knew the United States was beginning to pull out of the war, and they were afraid that they might be killed before their tour ended. This fear sometimes led to a terrible and desperate act called fragging. Fragging was the attempt to kill a commanding officer with a fragmentation grenade, usually while he slept. Some fragging incidents occurred because soldiers believed an officer was making the troops take risks that could get them killed. More often, it happened after an individual's disagreement with a superior officer. An estimated 730 suspected fragging incidents occurred between 1969 and 1972. More than 700 were injured and at least 86 officers died. While similar murders also occurred in other wars, it was more common in Vietnam.

Bomb craters on the Ho Chi Minh Trail

credit: U.S. Air Force

John Kerry (1943–), who was later a U.S. senator and secretary of state, served as a naval lieutenant in the Vietnam War. In April 1971, he spoke at the Washington protest. Read a text of his speech at this website. If you were a soldier in Vietnam at the time, what might you have felt and thought on hearing his words?

 Kerry VVAW

The 45-day operation was a disaster. North Vietnamese forces had been expecting a mission such as this, and were prepared with tens of thousands of troops. The South Vietnamese troops advanced hesitatingly. As the communists struck, thousands of South Vietnamese fled in retreat. American airpower saved the operation from being a complete defeat, although all sides suffered significant losses. In the end, the Ho Chi Minh Trail remained in operation.

Weeks later, Nixon publicly declared Vietnamization a success.

THE PENTAGON PAPERS

Antiwar protests continued through 1971. On April 23, about 1,000 Vietnam veterans demonstrated in Washington, DC, along with 200,000 other protesters. Disillusioned and angry, the vets marched to the Capitol and threw their combat ribbons, helmets, and other war-related keepsakes on the Capitol steps. Their presence helped legitimize the antiwar protesters' cause. Two months later, something happened that gave protestors even more justification.

On June 13, *The New York Times* published an excerpt of a top-secret, 7,000-page Defense Department study tracking the development of the Vietnam War from 1945 to 1967. Known as the Pentagon Papers, the study had been prepared by Defense Department analysts at the request of former Secretary of Defense Robert McNamara.

The papers revealed the shocking extent to which the government had misled the public about the war.

For the first time, the American public learned that President Truman helped fund the French Indochina War, that Eisenhower had made it a goal to prevent a communist victory in the Vietnam-wide elections outlined in the Geneva Accords, and that the Kennedy administration was involved in Diem's overthrow. The papers also showed the war's goal had become primarily about avoiding a humiliating U.S. defeat, not preventing the spread of communism.

Perhaps most shocking for the public, the Pentagon Papers revealed that President Johnson had repeatedly deceived the public about his intention to limit the war. He had ignored CIA advice that escalating the war was likely to be unsuccessful.

Although the Nixon administration wasn't implicated by the papers, National Security Advisor Kissinger persuaded Nixon to object to the publication of further excerpts. He argued that they weakened the public faith in the president and might encourage other leaks. The Department of Justice quickly filed for a court injunction to prevent *The New York Times* from publishing further excepts. The case went to the U.S. Supreme Court within weeks.

DANIEL ELLSBERG (1931-)

The Pentagon Papers were illegally leaked by Daniel Ellsberg, a young military analyst who helped prepare the study. Ellsberg initially supported the war, but grew to deeply oppose it. After the papers were published, Ellsberg turned himself in to the authorities. His case went to trial, but a mistrial was declared when it was discovered that President Nixon attempted to discredit Ellsberg by having a team of former intelligence agents secretly break into Ellsberg's psychiatrist's office to find damaging information on him. This illegal break-in was one of the first steps toward the Watergate scandal, which ended Nixon's presidency.

In a 6-to-3 vote, the Supreme Court allowed the Pentagon Papers to be published. The court reasoned that the government had failed to meet the "heavy burden" that would justify imposing a prior restraint. This meant that the government had the legal duty to prove that it had extremely good reasons for restricting free speech, but hadn't done so. Following the court decision, *The New York Times* and multiple other newspapers printed installments of the papers.[4]

KISSINGER'S PEACE TALKS

Amid the Pentagon Papers fallout, the United States was still trying to negotiate peace. The formal talks in Paris had been deadlocked since late 1969, but secret negotiations between Henry Kissinger and Le Duc Tho (1911–1990), a leading member of the Hanoi politburo, inched the two nations closer to agreement. By late 1972, circumstances had changed enough that both sides were ready to bend.

In March 1972, the communists launched a massive attack on South Vietnam, known as the Eastertide Offensive. Led by General Giap, who had led the Viet Minh to victory over the French, the communists hoped to have the kind of decisive win they had scored at Dien Bien Phu. But after months of fierce fighting, the United States and South Vietnamese triumphed. The Eastertide Offensive's failure is believed to have made North Vietnam more willing to negotiate.

Kissinger wanted Nixon to have the war behind him before the November presidential elections. Nixon had already impressed the American public as a peacemaker by reopening communication with China and thawing the relationship with the Soviet Union. Bringing the troops home from Vietnam would be just the boost Nixon needed to win reelection.

STRATEGY FACT

People who opposed the war felt vindicated by the Pentagon Papers. The study was direct proof of the credibility gap between the government's actions and words.

By October, North Vietnam stopped insisting that President Thieu step down. Instead, the North proposed a national reconciliation council, in which North and South Vietnam would peacefully decide upon a political order for South Vietnam. They also agreed to a cease-fire and an exchange of POWs. The one thing Le Duc Tho refused to negotiate was the withdrawal of the 150,000 North Vietnamese troops from South Vietnam.

Kissinger gave in. Although he knew allowing North Vietnamese troops to stay would almost certainly mean the eventual downfall of South Vietnam, he believed that without this concession, an agreement would never be reached. He told others privately that he hoped for a "decent interval"—perhaps a year or two—after the agreement was signed before South Vietnam fell. That way, its collapse would not reflect badly on Nixon.

North Vietnam and the United States arrived at a draft agreement in October 1972. But when President Thieu saw the terms of the agreement, he was furious. He felt the United States had betrayed him, particularly by allowing North Vietnamese troops to remain in South Vietnam. He refused to sign the agreement and proposed numerous sweeping amendments. Kissinger presented the changes to Le Duc Tho, who was also furious. Negotiations continued for weeks, straight through the elections, which Nixon won easily.

To pressure North Vietnam, Nixon authorized an intense bombing campaign, nicknamed the "Christmas Bombings." In late December, 20,000 tons of bombs were dropped on heavily populated areas of North Vietnam for 11 days, killing 1,300 North Vietnamese civilians. Shortly afterward, North Vietnam resumed negotiations.

Listen to a recording of Nixon and Kissinger's conversation about negotiations and the probability of South Vietnam's fall. How does Nixon justify the moral dilemma they face? Consider why you agree or disagree.

 Nixon Kissinger conversations

B-52 crews being briefed for the Christmas Bombings

credit: U.S. Air Force

STRATEGY FACT

Kissinger and Le Duc Tho were awarded the 1973 Nobel Peace Prize for arranging the cease-fire in the Vietnam War. Tho refused to accept the prize. Kissinger accepted it, but offered to return it when Saigon fell in 1975.

To get Thieu on board, Nixon and Kissinger secretly promised him that if North Vietnam broke the agreement, the United States would return to take "swift and severe retaliatory action" against it. In addition, they promised that the United States would give South Vietnam $1 billion in aid. Thieu reluctantly agreed to sign the agreement, though it was very similar to the one he'd strongly rejected earlier.[5]

On January 27, 1973, the United States, North Vietnam, and South Vietnam signed the Paris Peace Accords. Two months later, nearly 600 POWs were released, and the last American combat troops came home. For the Americans, the war had finally ended.

Not so for the Vietnamese.

THE DECENT INTERVAL

Nixon couldn't keep his promises to President Thieu. In August 1973, Congress banned the funding of any further military involvement in Indochina without congressional approval. A year later, Congress also reduced the amount of financial aid to South Vietnam from $1 billion to $700 million. Of this, South Vietnam received only about $400 million.

Nixon and Kissinger were upset by this. They wanted to honor their promises and thought breaking them reflected badly on the United States. But Nixon was in no position to argue. He was facing impeachment for having helped cover up a break-in of the offices of the Democratic National Committee in the Watergate building during his reelection campaign.

Rather than be impeached, Nixon resigned from the presidency on August 9, 1974. Vice President Gerald Ford (1913–2006) immediately took his place.

Richard Nixon leaving the White House after resigning

credit: Oliver F. Atkins

WATERGATE SCANDAL

On June 17, 1972, five men were caught breaking into the Democratic National Headquarters in the Watergate building in Washington, DC. Investigations revealed they were members of a committee to help get President Nixon reelected, and that they had stolen top-secret documents and placed illegal listening devices in the Democratic Party's offices. Although Nixon insisted that the White House was not involved with the burglary, tape-recorded conversations of White House officials showed that Nixon knew of the crime and had tried to cover it up. When the truth came to light, Nixon resigned, the only U.S. president to do so. You can listen to part of the Watergate hearings. How do you think Americans felt about the hearings?

🔎 PBS Watergate hearings

STRATEGY FACT

As communist troops drew closer, President Thieu resigned from the presidency at the urging of the U.S. ambassador. Aided by the CIA, Thieu fled to safety in Taiwan with bitter words for the United States on his lips.

You can see pictures and read first-hand accounts of the evacuation of Saigon at the *Newsweek* website. How might it have felt to be one of the last people evacuated? How might it have felt to be left behind?

Newsweek evacuate Saigon

Meanwhile, both North and South Vietnam violated the Peace Accords by continuing to fight. And North Vietnam quietly began to plan for a major offensive to regain South Vietnam.

THE FALL OF SAIGON

In January 1975, the North Vietnamese army began steadily advancing toward Saigon in the Spring Offensive. At first, the South Vietnamese army tried to repel them, but soon began to flee. President Thieu anxiously reminded President Ford of the promises made to him before signing the Peace Accords, and asked for U.S. assistance. Ford asked Congress to increase aid to South Vietnam by $300 million—he was refused.

By April 27, North Vietnamese troops had surrounded a chaotic Saigon. Two days later, President Ford authorized the U.S. Navy to evacuate all remaining American personnel, their relatives, and certain South Vietnamese citizens in Saigon. Some 1,300 Americans and 5,500 South Vietnamese were airlifted from the city within 18 hours.[6]

On April 30, just after the last American helicopter left the embassy, communist tanks crashed through the gates of the presidential palace in Saigon. Soon, the North Vietnamese flag was flying high. South Vietnam promptly surrendered and the 20-year war was over.

KEY QUESTIONS

- Who do you think are the "silent majority" in today's society?
- Do you think the U.S. government is more forthcoming with information today?
- Did President Nixon achieve "peace with honor?" Why or why not?

BLOWING THE WHISTLE

Daniel Ellsberg, the man who released the Pentagon Papers, was the first major whistle-blower of the modern era. A whistle-blower is defined as a person who informs on a person or organization believed to be engaging in immoral, unethical, or illegal behavior. Whistle-blowers are usually protected by federal law, so they can report unethical actions without fear of getting into trouble. But such laws generally don't protect those who reveal classified government information. Ellsberg did so knowing he could be jailed for life. Some Americans regarded him as a hero, while others viewed him as a traitor.

- **Learn more about Ellsberg's motivations by reading the transcript of his interview with Walter Cronkite, which was held shortly after the release of the Pentagon Papers.**

   Ellsberg Cronkite interview

  - In what ways can whistle-blowing be beneficial to society?

  - In what ways can whistle-blowing be detrimental to society?

  - Do you think Ellsberg was a hero or a traitor? Explain.

  - Are there any circumstances where you might view a whistle-blower as the opposite of the answer you provided above? Describe.

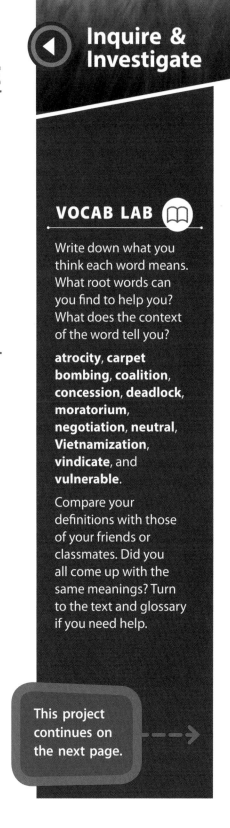

Inquire & Investigate

VOCAB LAB

Write down what you think each word means. What root words can you find to help you? What does the context of the word tell you?

atrocity, carpet bombing, coalition, concession, deadlock, moratorium, negotiation, neutral, Vietnamization, vindicate, and **vulnerable.**

Compare your definitions with those of your friends or classmates. Did you all come up with the same meanings? Turn to the text and glossary if you need help.

This project continues on the next page.

• **You can learn more about recent government whistle-blowers by researching Edward Snowden and Chelsea Manning.** Create a two-column, seven-row chart that compares and contrasts one whistle-blower with Daniel Ellsberg. Use the following questions as a guide.

  • How were the circumstances of each whistle-blower similar?

  • What were key differences in their situations?

  • What motivated each of them?

  • How did each of them reveal classified information?

  • What consequences did they suffer?

  • How were they perceived by the public?

  • Do you view one of them more favorably than the other? Why?

To investigate more, imagine that you have learned of an immoral, unethical, or illegal act that a person in authority, such as a teacher or club leader, is committing. Map out three different ways you could respond to the situation. Consider whom you might tell, evidence you might need, the potential consequences you might face, and the possible consequences of doing nothing. Of the three, which response would you be most likely to take?

Chapter 6 ▶
War's Aftermath

What can we learn from the Vietnam War?

Although the Vietnam War experience was traumatic for the United States, we are still in danger of repeating the same mistakes.

The Vietnam War ended decades ago, but its ripples are still felt today. That 58,220 Americans and as many as 3 million Vietnamese lost their lives was just the beginning of the war's legacy. The conflict changed U.S. foreign policy, damaged the economy, created thousands of wounded veterans, and left a public distrusting its government.

And that was minor compared to the devastation Vietnam faced. Both North and South Vietnam suffered devastatingly losses during the war. In addition to the deaths of millions of people, hundreds of thousands more were displaced from their homes and villages.

If these lessons are ignored, we risk experiencing another Vietnam in the future.

AMERICA'S WOUNDS

The America that emerged from the Vietnam War in 1975 was greatly changed from the country that existed in 1955, when the United States first involved itself in Vietnam. Before Vietnam, most Americans had believed in U.S. invincibility. They thought the combined power of the American government, military, and economy made the United States impossible to defeat.

Afterward, they knew better. No matter how the issue was spun, it was clear that the United States had failed to achieve its goals in Vietnam. The communists, that long-hated enemy, had won.

The Vietnam conflict also shook Americans' faith in their public institutions. Accustomed to seeing themselves as the good guys in military conflicts, most Americans felt this war had created too much ugliness to look upon it with pride.

> Many people now viewed politicians and the military with skepticism and mistrust.

The weakened economy didn't help the national mood. The United States spent approximately $168 billion on the war in Vietnam. Fearing public backlash, President Johnson had been determined to finance both the war and Great Society programs without raising taxes in any significant way. This resulted in enormous inflation in the 1970s, which decreased the standard of living of many Americans.

Faced with so much negativity, Americans seemed to develop a collective amnesia about the war. Despite the continuing turmoil overseas, stories about it dropped from newspaper headlines, and few people were willing to discuss Vietnam.

Just one week before Saigon fell in April 1975, President Gerald Ford gave a speech to students at Tulane University. How did he set the tone for the way Americans processed the Vietnam War? How might a Vietnam veteran have responded to these remarks? How might South Vietnam?

 Ford address Tulane

Newly freed POWs heading back to the United States in 1973

credit: U.S. Air Force

THE VETS' RETURN

When the last U.S. soldiers came home from Vietnam in 1973, their families rejoiced, but there were no celebratory parades as there had been after earlier wars. Instead, veterans felt an uneasy silence or even outright hostility. Some people blamed the soldiers for the ugliness and failures of the war. Numerous vets have shared stories of being called "baby-killer" and of suffering cruel taunts and harassment by strangers who recognized their military haircuts or uniforms.

Worse, vets felt abandoned by the very government that had sent them to war. No effort was made to help them readjust to civilian life, which now seemed strange and unfamiliar to many. There were few government programs in place to help the young men find jobs in the difficult economy or to continue their education. There was no plan to help them reconcile their service to their country with a war that no one wanted to talk about. Many vets felt as though their experiences and sacrifices were meaningless.

STRATEGY FACT

It's commonly believed that Vietnam vets were spat upon by demonstrators after returning home from the war. But Jerry Lembcke, Vietnam veteran and author of the book, *The Spitting Image*, was unable to find a single recorded incidence of a soldier being spat upon. Although it might have happened, it was a rare occurrence.

Vietnam vets also had to face a persistent stereotype that they were crazed, drug-addicted, or violent men incapable of functioning in regular society. The truth is that while many vets did struggle to adjust after the war, the vast majority reintegrated well into civilian life.

Integration wasn't always smooth, however. Some vets kept their war service secret from new friends and colleagues. Others blocked the entire experience from their minds, finding it easier to join in the national amnesia than to try to make others understand their experiences.

A SHATTERED VIETNAM

In Vietnam, no one could forget the war. Two decades of fighting had left the country physically and economically ravaged, particularly in the south.

The United States had dropped nearly 14 million tons of bombs, destroying immense areas of farmland and approximately two-thirds of its villages. Once-green hills and rice paddies were punctured with enormous craters, and thousands of square miles of forests had been reduced to blackened, stumpy ruins. In the north, the infrastructure of targeted cities had been devastated.

The war also left behind hundreds of thousands of injured soldiers and citizens, more than 800,000 orphans, a million widows, and 500,000 acres of cropland thoroughly polluted by Agent Orange and other herbicides. People who attempted to work the land risked death, as the countryside was still riddled with unexploded bombs and mines. The country also faced a growing health crisis as peasants exposed to Agent Orange developed a variety of serious health conditions and babies were born with birth defects.

A helicopter spraying a defoliation agent on agricultural land during the war

credit: Brian K. Grigsby, SPC5

In addition to coping with these difficult conditions, the South Vietnamese had to adjust to life under a communist government. It was a dramatic change. When the communists took over Saigon, which they promptly renamed Ho Chi Minh City, their immediate goal was to convert the South Vietnamese to the communist agenda.

Between 500,000 and 1 million South Vietnamese men were sent to re-education camps. In reality, these were labor camps where the men were made to work for years under inhumane conditions. More than 165,000 people are estimated to have died in these camps, most likely from starvation and disease.

South Vietnamese outside the camps also suffered. The South's economy had been bolstered by the American presence during the war. Once U.S. troops left, many jobs and businesses that catered to the military dried up, and the quality of life worsened.

After Saigon fell, living conditions tumbled even further as the government took control of all private businesses and redistributed a portion of the population to the decimated countryside. The South Vietnamese lost their freedom to act, own certain possessions, and earn money as they liked. Questioning of government policies was forbidden.

Communist officials and their informants were constantly watching to make sure everyone complied with the law. How would you feel living under these circumstances?

Finding these oppressive conditions intolerable, more than a million South Vietnamese fled the country between 1975 and the mid-1980s. People who could scrape together the money bribed officials or paid for fake identity documents to get out. Others stowed away on fishing vessels or even created makeshift boats.

Commonly known as boat people because most fled by sea, the refugees who safely escaped landed in refugee camps in other Asian countries, including Hong Kong, Malaysia, Singapore, and Thailand. From there many moved on to the United States, France, Canada, Australia, and other countries.

ATTEMPTS TO HEAL

The late 1970s saw America take small steps toward healing the country's pain and division over Vietnam. In January 1977, Jimmy Carter (1924–), the new president, offered non-violent draft evaders a full pardon, thinking it would help put the war in the past. The pardon cleared about 11,600 draft evaders who were under indictment or who already had been convicted of draft evasion. The pardon also allowed hundreds of thousands of men who had fled the country to return to the United States without fear of prosecution.

Most draft evaders who had fled the country came home after the war, but about 50,000 remained in Canada.

In 1979, Vietnam veteran activists formed the Vietnam Veterans of America to advocate for their needs. Among other things, the organization helped vets push for favorable veteran-related legislation, educated them on the effects of Agent Orange and PTSD, and kept them informed about their rights to certain benefits. The organization remains active today in helping vets and their families.

As national reflection on the Vietnam War increased, writers, artists, and filmmakers began to interpret the war experience. The late 1970s and 1980s saw a flood of blockbuster films about the war, including *The Deer Hunter*, *Apocalypse Now*, *Platoon*, and *Rambo: First Blood*. Although some of these portrayed combat soldiers sympathetically, many simply reinforced stereotypes of Vietnam vets as very damaged people.

The literature that emerged offered less sensational views of the war. Some Vietnam vets began to write to try to make sense of their experience, as did many journalists who witnessed the war. Their books helped the public understand the war in a more personal way.

Journalist Michael Herr's (1940–2016) memoir, *Dispatches*, published in 1977, is widely known as one of the finest books on the war. You can read an excerpt of *Dispatches* at this website. What are some of the different feelings the characters had about the war? Is there anything that surprised you?

 NPR
Dispatches

THE VIETNAM MEMORIAL

The most significant event to help bring healing to America and show appreciation for the veterans was the creation of the Vietnam Veterans Memorial. The idea was the brainchild of Vietnam veteran Jan Scruggs (1950–), who had fought in the war fresh out of high school. In 1979, he and others created the Vietnam Veterans Memorial Fund, and raised more than $8 million entirely from private donors.

In 1980, the memorial fund organized a nationwide design competition. The eight-person jury assessed 1,400 entries and unanimously selected a simple, abstract design of a wall. The jury was stunned to learn the design was created by a 21-year-old Yale University student, Maya Lin (1959–).

The Memorial Wall consists of two simple slabs of polished black granite engraved with the names of every soldier who died or went missing in Vietnam. They are listed in chronological order by year. The wall starts out at knee-height, with the names of those first killed in the war. As you walk its length, the ground slopes slightly downward as the dense wall of names rises upward. As you approach the end, the wall again slopes downward and the flow of names trickles to an end.

Even this tribute was not free of controversy. Many people were outraged at the not-yet-erected design, calling it an ugly gash, while others condemned it for being black, the so-called color of shame. Still others complained that it only honored dead veterans and had no heroic messages or symbols. Some people called Lin, who is of Chinese descent, a communist and alleged that there was a communist on the jury, which triggered a brief investigation.

GUERRILLA VS. CONVENTIONAL

The war in Vietnam was fought with guerrilla tactics instead of conventional warfare, which the United States was more used to. In conventional warfare, the fighting occurs between two fairly organized, easily identifiable groups of people. In guerrilla fighting, people who seem like civilians might actually be the enemy. This was a new experience for U.S. soldiers, one that required different skills and resilience to be successful.

credit: Michael J. Carden, U.S. Defense Department

To accommodate these concerns, an American flag and a bronze statue of three soldiers were placed in a little wooded area opposite the wall.

On November 13, 1982, the wall was dedicated before a crowd of 150,000 people. Within weeks, public opinion about the wall shifted radically. Veterans and family members approached the wall in tears as they looked for the names of loved ones that the war had taken. They lovingly touched and made pencil rubbings of the engravings, pointed out names to young children, knelt in prayer, and sobbed in grief. They left heaps of flowers, letters, photos, and other mementos at its base. To this day, it is one of the most visited sites in Washington, DC, and a revered and sacred place to remember the most heartbreaking legacy of the war.

MOVING FORWARD

As time passed, the United States and Vietnam gradually began to heal their relationship, although it was understandably difficult at first. After the communists took over South Vietnam in 1975, the United States quickly imposed a trade embargo on the unified country and refused to give it the reconstruction aid that had been promised in the Peace Accords.

Relations between the two countries were further strained by the United States' concern that Vietnam was still holding captive POWs and soldiers missing in action (MIAs). Some witnesses claimed to have seen Americans held in the jungle. For nearly two decades, the Defense Intelligence Agency investigated the matter, assessed the credibility of the witnesses, and tried to get answers from officials in Vietnam.

In 1993, the Senate Select Committee on POW/MIA Affairs did a final assessment. After reviewing more than 1 million documents on the matter, it was determined in 1991 that there was no credible evidence of POW/MIAs still in Vietnam.

> Today, roughly 644 Vietnam War soldiers are still not accounted for.

By 1986, Vietnam realized that its centralized economy wasn't working. It began moving toward a socialist economic system that encouraged private business and foreign investment. By 1994, the country had progressed enough for President Bill Clinton (1946–) to lift the 19-year trade ban against Vietnam. He normalized diplomatic relations with the country the following year.

STRATEGY FACT

MIAs are not unusual in war. World War II had more than 78,000 American MIAs, while Korea had 8,177.

SENATE INVESTIGATION

The Senate Select Committee on POW/MIA Affairs was led by Vietnam veteran Senator John Kerry. Also on the committee was John McCain (1936–), a U.S. senator from Arizona and presidential candidate in 2008. McCain was a Navy pilot in Vietnam who had been shot down, captured, imprisoned, and tortured in the prison called the Hanoi Hilton for five years.

credit: Arianos

VIETNAM TODAY

Vietnam of the twenty-first century is greatly changed from the Vietnam of the 1960s, when the war was at its height. Today, the country welcomes more than 6 million tourists a year to sun themselves on its sandy beaches and marvel at its dramatic landscapes. You can even go on tours of the Cu Chi tunnels or take a boat tour of the Mekong Delta. Here is an article describing today's youth in Vietnam and their perspective on the war.

What do you have in common with the youth of Vietnam? What are your differences? What might Ho Chi Minh think about today's Vietnam? How about the U.S. presidents involved in the war?

 L.A. Times
Vietnam
future

In 2007, Vietnam became a member of the World Trade Organization. American exports to Vietnam grew from $1.4 billion that year to $9.6 billion in 2016. Vietnam is still communist, but it is considered the most pro-American country in Southeast Asia. A 2015 poll showed that 76 percent of Vietnamese view the United States favorably, and countless U.S. travelers say the Vietnamese are friendly to Americans and harbor no ill-will.

VIETNAM'S LEGACY

Nearly a half-century has passed since Saigon fell, and the Vietnam War seems very distant. Yet it has left an imprint on American society, policies, and laws. For example, it is largely thanks to the Vietnam War that the legal voting age was lowered from 21 to 18. Teenage student protesters had strongly argued that if they were old enough to fight, they were also old enough to vote. Many high-ranking politicians agreed. Congress ratified the Twenty-sixth Amendment to the Constitution, which secured these rights, in 1971.

The Vietnam War also affected how conflicts that involve U.S. troops are now shown on television. The military is careful of how war is portrayed by the media and imposes strict censorship. Journalists today have limited access to battlefields and conflict zones, and some photographs are censored, particularly those of death or destruction caused by the U.S. military.

The biggest legacy of the Vietnam War is U.S. foreign policy. After the war ended, the United States became very hesitant to commit ground troops to any combat situation overseas. Despite having the world's biggest military with the most powerful weapons, the United States, for the first time, doubted whether that would be enough. Politicians feared ending up in another Vietnam, meaning a lengthy war with ever-increasing loss of American lives, vague objectives, and an unhappy public. This fear, doubt, and reluctance to act militarily was called the Vietnam Syndrome.

The Vietnam Syndrome was said to have ended with the first Gulf War in 1990. Then, it was declared definitely dead with President George W. Bush's (1946–) offensive actions in Afghanistan and Iraq. But some declared the syndrome was back with President Obama's (1961–) cautious foreign policy and refusal to commit troops to the Syrian conflict. In reality, the Vietnam War will likely continue to haunt U.S. foreign policy for decades to come.

LESSONS LEARNED

The Vietnam War is commonly described as a tragic and senseless conflict. It's almost impossible to find any positive benefits the war brought to the United States or the world. The war won't have been a complete waste of lives and potential, however, if we pay attention to its lessons.

You can watch Vietnam veteran Tim Keenan's return to Vietnam after 40 years. How were his emotions during the war different from his emotions on returning in peace time?

WARNING: This video uses strong language.

 Tim Keenan Naneek

The United States has been involved in two complex and lengthy wars during the twenty-first century: in Afghanistan and Iraq. Both are often compared to Vietnam for multiple reasons.

KEY QUESTIONS

- What do you think is the most tragic aspect of the Vietnam War?

- Is there anything an individual can do to avoid another conflict like Vietnam? What?

- What role has the youth vote played in elections since 1971?

Vietnam showed us how much harder it is to exit a war than to enter one. Because of the lack of well-defined objectives and an exit plan, the government spent more than half of the U.S. military involvement in Vietnam trying to figure out how to extricate itself. As politicians fretted over the appropriate exit strategy, more than 20,000 U.S. troops died.

The conflict also revealed the importance of knowing the nature of the war being fought. For North Vietnam and the Vietcong, the war meant one thing. For the United States, it meant something else. This led U.S. officials to underestimate the communists' resolve, motivation, and capabilities.

We must examine with clear eyes the history and motivation of our opponents.

It's crucial to know exactly what they're fighting for and what they're willing to risk for success. This must be weighed particularly against our own motivations and the level of risk we're willing to accept.

Finally, the Vietnam War should remind us of our shared humanity. This was the most bitter of conflicts. The loss of life and suffering that occurred on all sides was terrible. And yet today, the United States and Vietnam have a friendly relationship, despite Vietnam having a communist government. Many Vietnam vets have returned to Vietnam to seek reconciliation and peace. Some have even shared meals with former Vietnamese enemies and marveled at their wartime experience.

As war continues to rage in our world, Vietnam should remind us that in the end, we have more in common than that which sets us apart.

MEMORIALIZED

While the Vietnam Memorial Wall in Washington, DC, is the most famous memorial for Vietnam veterans, there are several other memorials across the country. These often feature a stone wall or plaque with the names of locals who perished in the war or a statue of a soldier.

- **Artist Chris Burden (1946–2015) created a work called "The Other Vietnam Memorial," which sits in the Museum of Contemporary Art in Chicago.** It is a steel installation with 13-foot copper plates inscribed with 3 million Vietnamese names. You can view this work at this webpage. What makes this work a piece of art in addition to a memorial?

🔍 Chris Burden

- **Create either a memorial for Vietnam veterans or a work of art in tribute to another aspect of the Vietnam War.** Consider the following.

  - What medium and materials will you use?

  - Who is your audience?

  - What kind of setting would you want for the memorial or art work? Why?

  - What feelings would you want the memorial or work of art to evoke?

> **To investigate more,** consider refugees who are fleeing their country today. What are their nationalities or ethnic groups? What are they fleeing? Does anyone have a moral obligation to assist them? Why or why not? What can you do to help refugees?

THE LONGEST WARS

The war in Afghanistan has replaced the Vietnam War as the United States' longest war. For this reason and others, it often is compared to the Vietnam War. But just how similar are the two wars?

- **Research online and in newspapers or magazines the history and development of the war in Afghanistan and compare it to what you have learned about the Vietnam War.** In conducting your research, consider the following.

  - the origins of the wars

  - the setting of the wars

  - the parties involved in the fighting

  - the motivations and objectives of each nation or political group involved

  - public opinion toward the war

  - the results of each war

- **After you've researched the issue, decide whether the war in Afghanistan is similar to Vietnam or not.** Compare and contrast your conclusions with a classmate.

> **To investigate more,** research the Iraq War, another long-term war that the United States is still fighting. What are some of the similarities and differences of this war to the Vietnam War? To the war in Afghanistan? How do these wars highlight what we still have to learn about entering foreign wars?

abdicate: to give up or renounce one's throne.

activist: a forceful supporter of a cause.

administration: a group that helps carry out the executive duties of a government.

alias: another name someone is known by.

alliance: a partnership formed for mutual benefit, especially between countries or organizations.

allies: people, groups, or countries that agree to help each other. The Allies refers to the United States, Great Britain, and other countries that fought together against the Germans during World War II.

ambush: to surprise attack someone from a hidden place.

amendment: a change made to a law or document.

amnesia: a type of severe memory loss.

ancestor: a person from whom one is descended, such as a great-grandmother.

animosity: strong hostility.

annihilation: the complete destruction of something.

anti-colonial: a person or country that opposes colonization.

artillery: mounted firearms such as missile-launchers.

assassinate: to kill a leader.

assimilation: to integrate people, ideas, and customs into a society.

atrocity: a cruel act of violence.

attrition: a wearing down or weakening of resistance, especially as a result of continuous pressure.

authority: the power or right to give orders, make decisions, and enforce the laws.

authorize: to give others the power or right to do something.

battalion: a large body of troops ready for battle.

BCE: put after a date, BCE stands for Before Common Era and counts down to zero. CE stands for Common Era and counts up from zero. These non-religious terms correspond to BC and AD. This book was printed in 2018 CE.

besiege: to attack vigorously.

Black Power Movement: a political and social movement aimed at helping African-Americans gain full equality with Caucasians.

Buddhist: a follower of Buddhism, a religion and philosophy common throughout Southeast Asia that believes the way to be free from suffering in life is through wisdom, concentration, and virtue.

capitalism: an economy in which people, not the government, own the factories, ships, and land used in the production and distribution of goods.

carpet bombing: to drop bombs all over a particular area so it will be completely destroyed.

casualty: a person, usually in the military, who died due to wounds, sickness, capture or other injury.

Catholic: a branch of Christianity.

censorship: when the government blocks citizens from seeing certain information.

civil rights: the rights to full legal, social and economic equality.

Civil Rights Movement: a national movement for racial equality in the 1950s and 1960s.

civil: of, relating to, or consisting of citizens.

civil war: a war between opposing groups of citizens of the same country.

civilian: anyone who is not on active duty in the military or police force.

civilization: a society having a relatively high level of cultural and technological development.

classified: information kept secret for reasons of national security.

coalition: a combination or alliance, especially a temporary one between persons, groups, or states.

Cold War: A period of high tension between democratic Western countries and communist countries in the East.

colonization: the action or process of settling among and establishing control over the people of an area.

commissioner: an official in charge of a government department.

communism: an economy in which the government owns everything used in the production and distribution of goods.

GLOSSARY

communist sympathizer: a person who is not communist but supports those who are.

complexity: the nature of something being complicated and difficult to understand or explain.

concession: to yield or give up a right, privilege, or point in an argument.

condemnation: the act of expressing strong disapproval or unfavorable judgment of something or someone.

conflict: a fight or strong disagreement.

conscientious objector: a person who refuses to serve in a military conflict or carry weapons for moral or religious reasons.

conscription: the required enrollment of people for military service.

containment: the action of keeping something harmful under control or within limits.

controversial: causing the public to argue over the issue.

corrupt: the dishonest or illegal behavior of people in power.

coup: a sudden, violent, and illegal seizure of power from a government.

court injunction: an order from a court that tells someone to do or not do a certain act.

covert: concealed or secret.

credibility: that someone or something is believable or trustworthy.

crop: a plant product that is grown from the ground and harvested.

cultivate: to prepare and use land for growing food.

culture: the customary behaviors and beliefs of an ethnic, racial, or social group.

cynical: distrustful of human sincerity or integrity.

deadlock: a state in which progress between two opposing forces is not possible.

debate: a discussion between people with differing viewpoints.

decimate: to kill a large number of something or to reduce something greatly.

declassified: to officially declare that certain political or military information is no longer secret.

defector: a person who deserts a cause or country to adopt another.

deferment: a temporary delay in taking someone in the military forces.

defoliation: to make leaves drop off a plant or trees, especially by using strong chemicals.

delegate: a person sent to a meeting as a representative of a larger group of people or a specific area of the country.

democracy: a form of government in which all people can vote for representatives.

democratic: supporting democracy and its principles of freedom.

demoralize: to take away the positive attitude or feelings of a person.

denunciation: public criticism of something or someone.

deplete: to use up, drain, or empty.

depose: to remove from a high office or position.

dictatorship: a government by a dictator with absolute rule over the people.

diplomat: someone who represents a country.

disarmament: to reduce or withdraw military forces and weapons.

disillusioned: feeling disappointment from finding out that something isn't as good as it was thought to be.

disproportionate: too large or too small compared to something else.

dissent: to disagree with a widely held opinion.

distinctive: an aspect of something that makes it stand out as special or unique.

divisive: creating disunity or extreme disagreement.

documentary: a factual movie or television program.

domestic: existing or occurring inside a particular country.

domino theory: the idea that if one country became communist neighboring countries would also.

GLOSSARY

draft dodger: a person who tries to avoid being required to join the military.

draft: a government requirement that men join the military.

dynasty: a powerful family or group that rules for many years.

economic: something that relates to the production of money, wealth, and goods.

economy: a system of producing and consuming goods and services.

editorial: an article in a newspaper or publication that expresses someone's opinion.

elongate: drawn out in length.

embargo: an order to temporarily stop something, especially trading or information.

emotion: strong feelings such as love or anger.

emphasis: special importance.

encroachment: intrusion on someone's territory or rights.

envoy: someone who is sent as a representative of one government to another.

era: a period of time marked by a particular set of events.

erosion: the gradual wearing away.

escalate: to increase.

ethnic: referring to the shared origin, characteristics, and culture of a certain group of people.

evacuate: to move from a dangerous place to a safe one.

excessive: too much of something.

exile: to be sent away or kept away from your own country.

explicit: to be clear and exact.

exploit: to use and benefit from something. Also to benefit unfairly from someone else's work.

export: any good or service that is shipped outside the country or brings in money from other countries.

extricate: to release or free something from an entanglement.

fascist: a follower of a dictator who holds absolute power over a country.

feign: to pretend to have a particular problem or feeling.

fervent: having great intensity of feeling.

figurehead: a leader without real power.

flounder: to struggle.

fluent: able to express oneself easily in another language.

foe: an enemy or opponent.

foreign policy: the way the government deals with other nations.

fruitless: failing to achieve the desired results.

futile: pointless.

garrison: a military post where troops are stationed.

goods: items for sale.

Great Society: the goals of President Lyndon Johnson to improve education, equalize racial inequality, and provide more healthcare to all members of society.

guerrilla warfare: a form of irregular warfare in which a small group of combatants uses ambushes, sabotage, raids, and hit-and-run tactics to fight a larger and less mobile traditional military.

guerrilla: a member of an unofficial military group.

herbicide: a chemical used to kill unwanted plants such as weeds.

heritage: something that is handed down from the past.

hippies: people, especially in the 1960s, who rejected established values and believed in promoting peace and love.

homosexual: a person who is sexually attracted to others of the same gender.

hostile: very unfriendly, relating to an enemy.

humanity: people in general or showing kindness to other people.

iconic: a widely recognized symbol of a certain time.

ideological: something based on a particular set of belief or ideas.

ideology: a system of ideas and ideals, especially one that forms the basis of economic or political theory and policy.

imminent: about to happen.

GLOSSARY

immoral: something outside a person's or society's standards for appropriate behavior.

impeach: to formally charge a public official with misconduct or a crime.

imperialism: a situation in which one country has a lot of power or influence over others, particularly in political and economic matters.

inaugural: having to do with a presidential inauguration. Also marking the beginning of something new.

incendiary: designed to cause fires.

indefinite: having no clearly defined boundaries.

independence: freedom from being ruled by another country.

indictment: a formal statement accusing someone of something.

Indochina: a former geographical name of the region now known as Southeast Asia.

induction: an occasion when someone is formally introduced to a new job or organization.

infiltrate: to join a group to spy on it or to sneak into a place to get information.

inflation: a continuing rise in the price of goods and services.

informant: someone who gives information to another person or organization.

infrastructure: the large-scale public systems, services, and facilities of a country or region, including power and water supplies, public transportation, telecommunications, roads, and schools.

inhumane: cruelty that causes people to suffer.

instability: the tendency to behave in an unpredictable or uncertain manner.

insurgent: a person who revolts against civil authority or an established government.

insurrection: an organized attempt by people to overthrow their government, usually by violence.

integrate: to become part of.

intellectual: involving serious thought. Also a highly educated person.

intervene: to alter the course of an event.

intimidation: the act of making another person fearful with threats or other shows of power.

investor: a person who gives a company money in exchange for future profits.

invincible: someone who cannot be defeated.

irrigate: to supply land with water using pipes and ditches, usually for crops.

justification: a fact, reason, or circumstance that explains some action or behavior.

labyrinth: a maze.

left-leaning: tending to have a politically liberal point of view.

legacy: the lasting influence of a person or thing.

legislation: new laws.

legitimize: to make something acceptable or legal.

liberal: respecting many different types of beliefs or behavior.

liberation: an occasion when something or someone is released from oppressive conditions.

liberty: the freedom to live as you wish or go where you want.

logistical: relating to the planning of an event to ensure that it goes smoothly.

looting: taking something by dishonesty, force, or stealth.

Marxism: the political, economic and social principles and policies advocated by Karl Marx, especially concerning the practice of socialism and the struggle of the working class to form a classless society.

meme: a cultural item in the form of an image, video, or phrase that is spread by the Internet and is altered in a humorous way.

memoir: the written story of an event or period of the author's life.

MIA: a soldier declared missing in action.

migrate: to move from one area to another.

military: the army or other part of the armed forces of a country.

GLOSSARY

militia: an army made up of citizens instead of professional soldiers.

mission: an important task or duty.

missionary: a member of a religious group that is sent into another area to spread the word about his or her religion's teachings and perform works of service.

mistrial: a trial that can't be completed, usually because of a legal mistake made.

momentum: a force that keeps an object moving after it has begun to move.

monarch: a king or queen.

monopoly: complete control of something, such as a service or product.

monsoon: a wind that brings heavy rainfall to southern Asia in summer.

moral: the discussion between what is right and what is wrong for a particular issue.

morale: feelings of enthusiasm and loyalty that a person or group has about a task or job.

moratorium: a temporary stopping of an activity.

myth: an ancient story or set of stories.

napalm: a substance containing petrol that burns strongly and is used in bombs.

nation: a country.

national identity: the cultures, traditions, language, and politics of a country.

national security: a term describing the defense and protection of the interests of a country.

nationalistic: supporting a belief that one's own country is superior to others, and placing primary emphasis on the promotion of its culture and interests.

Nazis: the main political party of Germany before and during World War II.

negotiation: working to reach an agreement, compromise, or treaty through bargaining and discussing.

neutral: not taking part in a dispute between others.

neutralize: to stop something from having an effect.

nuclear annihilation: complete destruction because of a nuclear weapon.

nuclear war: a war where deadly, radioactive missiles or bombs are used.

objective: a goal.

occupation: a job.

offensive: an attacking military campaign.

ominous: threatening, giving the impression that something bad is going to happen.

opposition: resistance or dissent, expressed in action or argument.

oppression: a situation where people are governed in an unfair or cruel way.

oust: to force someone to leave a position of power, job, or place.

pacification: the act of calming, appeasing, or suppressing a group that is upset or hostile.

pacifist: a person who is opposed to war or violence.

pacify: to make something or someone calm.

parallel: things that lie in the same direction or have the same nature or tendency.

paranoia: an extreme or unreasonable feeling that people are going to criticize you or hurt you.

pardon: to forgive someone for something they have done.

passive resistance: to show opposition a government or laws in a non-violent way.

patriotic: an act or statement inspired by the devotion to a person's country.

peasantry: a class of people who are small farmers or laborers of low social rank.

perpetuate: to cause something to continue.

persecution: a campaign to exterminate or drive away a group of people based on their religious beliefs or other characteristics.

perspective: a person's point of view.

pervasive: happening or existing among many people or places.

picket: to stand or march near a certain place to protest or persuade others not to enter.

philosophies: a particular system of thought based on study.

GLOSSARY

plains: a large area of flat land.

plantation: a large farm or estate where items such as cotton, tobacco, or cocoa are grown and harvested.

polarization: people or opinions divided into two opposing groups.

policy: a course of action decided upon and pursued by a government.

politburo: the main government group in a communist country.

political: relating to a country's government.

politicians: people who hold political office.

Posttraumatic Stress Disorder (PTSD): a psychological reaction to a stressful event that can involve depression, anxiety, flashbacks, and nightmares.

prejudice: having an unfair or unfavorable opinion or feeling, usually formed without knowledge, thought, or reason.

primary sources: firsthand accounts of events.

privileges: special benefits that one person or a group of persons enjoy over others.

profit: the amount gained by transferring something of value to someone else for more than it cost.

propaganda: information, especially of a biased or misleading nature, that is used to promote or publicize a particular political cause or point of view.

protectorate: a country controlled and defended by a more powerful country.

protest: a strong complaint expressing disagreement or disapproval of something.

province: a division of a country, similar to a state.

provisional: temporary, existing for the time being.

proxy war: a conflict between two states or non-state actors where neither entity directly engages the other.

public institution: an organization or business that is backed by public funds and controlled by the government.

puppet government: a government that seems to have authority over a country, but is actually controlled by another power.

racially: relating to race.

rampant: wild and out of control.

rebel: a person who resists against their government or other authority.

reconciliation: a situation where people who have argued put aside their differences and become friendly again.

recruit: to enlist someone into the armed forces.

referendum: a vote in which all people in a country or area give their opinions about a matter.

refinery: a factory where products in their natural state, such as sugar, are freed from impurities.

refugee: a person who has escaped their own country because of war or for political or economic reasons.

regime: a government, especially an authoritarian one.

reintegrate: to unite or bring a separate unit back into a whole.

renege: to fail to keep a promise or agreement.

repercussion: the effect or result of an event or action.

resistance: the act of opposing something.

resources: the wealth of a country or its means of producing wealth.

retaliate: to hurt or cause harm to someone because they have done something harmful to you.

revere: to deeply admire and respect someone.

revolution: an overthrow of an established government by the people governed.

rout: to defeat an enemy completely.

ruthlessness: not worrying about or thinking about any pain caused to others.

self-immolate: to set oneself on fire.

silent majority: a group of people who aren't outspoken and yet are believed to form a majority.

skepticism: doubting the truth or value of an idea or belief.

slave laborer: a person who is performing unpaid labor under threat.

sniper fire: gunshots fired by someone hidden.

social change: a change in social behavior, patterns, and values through time.

social reform: a type of social movement that aims to make gradual social changes through time.

socialism: the set of beliefs that all people are equal and should share equally in a country's money.

Southeast Asia: a sub-region of Asia, south of China, east of India, west of New Guinea, and north of Australia.

sovereign: having supreme or ultimate power.

Soviet Union: a communist-ruled union with a totalitarian regime that lasted from 1922 to 1991.

stalemate: a contest where neither side is winning.

stereotype: to make a judgment about a group of individuals.

strategic: helping to achieve a plan or result, especially in business, politics, or war.

stronghold: an area where most people have the same beliefs and values.

subservient: extremely and humbly obedient or yielding to the authority of another.

substantial: of considerable importance, size, or worth.

subversive: trying to destroy or damage something, especially a political system.

succumb: to give way to a superior force.

superiority: a higher quality, accomplishment, or significance.

suppressed: to have ended something with force.

surrogate: taking the place of somebody.

teach-in: a meeting held, usually on a college campus, to raise awareness of or express an opinion on an issue.

terraced: a series of horizontal ridges made in a hillside.

terrain: land or ground and all of its physical features, such as hills, rocks, and water.

territory: an area that is considered to belong to a country or government or people.

totalitarian: a system of government that has absolute control over its people and requires them to be completely obedient.

trade: the activity of buying and selling goods or services between people or countries.

traditions: a belief or way of acting that a particular group has followed for a long time.

traitor: a person who is not loyal to their country, social groups, or own beliefs.

trajectory: the curve or line taken by an object moving through space. Also the path of events.

traumatic: an event or experience that is psychologically painful.

treason: the crime of acting to harm your country, especially by helping the enemies of your country.

tribunal: a court of justice.

troops: a group of soldiers.

unanimous: having the agreement of everyone.

unconventional: not traditional.

undeterred: not wanting to give up.

unethical: morally wrong.

unprovoked: occurring without cause or justification.

uprising: an act of opposition against people in one area of a country against those in power.

veteran: someone who has served in the armed forces during the war.

Vietcong: Vietnamese communists in South Vietnam.

Vietnam Syndrome: a reference to the aversion of U.S. military involvements overseas.

Vietnamization: The U.S. policy of allowing South Vietnam to take the lead in the military fight against North Vietnam.

vindicate: to prove that someone is free from guilt, blame, or error.

vulnerable: susceptible to emotional or physical harm.

Watergate: a political scandal leading to the resignation of President Richard Nixon.

whistle-blower: a person who makes a public disclosure of corruption or wrongdoing.

zeal: enthusiasm.

RESOURCES

BOOKS

Appy, Christian G. *American Reckoning: The Vietnam War and Our National Identity*. Penguin Group, 2015.

DeBenedetti, Charles. *An American Ordeal: The Antiwar Movement of the Vietnam Era*. Syracuse University Press, 1990.

Karnow, Stanley. *Vietnam: A History: The First Complete Account of the War*. The Viking Press, 1983.

Hallin, Daniel C. *The Uncensored War: The Media and Vietnam*. University of California Press, first paperback printing, 1989.

Langguth, A.J. *Our Vietnam: The War 1954–1975*. Simon & Schuster, 2000.

McCormick, Anita Louise. *The Vietnam Antiwar Movement in American History*. Enslow Publishers, Inc., 2000.

McMaster, H.R. *Dereliction of Duty: Lyndon Johnson, Robert McNamara, the Joint Chiefs of Staff, and the Lies that Led to Vietnam*. HarperCollins, 1999.

The Vietnam War: The Definitive Illustrated History. DK Publishing, 2017.

Zullo, Allan. *Vietnam War Heroes (10 True Tales)*. Scholastic, 2014.

Eaton, Ed. *Mekong Mud Dogs: The Story of Sgt. Ed Eaton*. N.p., 2014.

WEBSITES

Office of the Historian. history.state.gov/milestones/1961-1968.
Official historians of the U.S. State Department provide a record of "Milestones" in U.S. foreign relations, including summaries of several key moments in the Vietnam War.

History. history.com/topics/vietnam-war/vietnam-war-history
This website offers articles, videos, speeches, and interactive graphics on the Vietnam War.

Stars and Stripes. www.stripes.com/news/special-reports/vietnam-at-50/1967.
This online military magazine provides a retrospective on the Vietnam War and examines its legacy from 1975 through today.

National Archives. archives.gov/research/vietnam-war.
The National Archives' website has thousands of primary sources from the Vietnam era, including photographs, letters, leaflets, draft cards, maps, etc.

National Public Radio. npr.org/tags/137148468/vietnam-war.
This website offers stories on Vietnam War-related news of today.

RESOURCES

SOURCE NOTES

CHAPTER 2

1 Yale Law School, Lillian Goldman Law Library. "President Harry S. Truman's Address Before a Joint Session of Congress, March 12, 1947." N.d. Retrieved from: avalon.law.yale.edu/20th_century/trudoc.asp.
2 The American Presidency Project. "President Dwight D. Eisenhower's News Conference, April 7, 1954." N.d. Retrieved from: presidency.ucsb.edu/ws/?pid=10202.
3 Thuylong1. "Madame Nhu's response to Thich Quang Duc." YouTube, August 11, 2011. Retrieved from: youtube.com/watch?v=d_PWM9gWR5E.

CHAPTER 3

1 Vescovi, C. "LBJ 'American boys....' " YouTube, March 4, 2011. Retrieved from: youtube.com/watch?v=1qj6MVGuX8E.
2 Ford, H. "Why CIA Analysts were so doubtful about Vietnam." Retrieved from: cia.gov/library/center-for-the-study-of-intelligence/csi-publications/csi-studies/studies/97unclass/vietnam.html. **and** Laurie, C. "CIA and the Wars in Southeast Asia, 1947-1975." September 2016. Retrieved from: cia.gov/library/center-for-the-study-of-intelligence/csi-publications/books-and-monographs/Anthology-CIA-and-the-Wars-in-Southeast-Asia/pdfs-1/vietnam-anthology-interactive.pdf.
3 Karnow, Stanley. *Vietnam: A History: The First Complete Account of the War*. The Viking Press, 1983. p. 463.

CHAPTER 4

1 "Memorandum From the President's Special Assistant for National Security Affairs to President Johnson." February 7, 1965. Retrieved from: presidency.ucsb.edu/vietnam/showdoc.php?docid=46.
2 Goodwin, G. "Black and White in Vietnam." *The New York Times*, July 18, 2017. Retrieved from: nytimes.com/2017/07/18/opinion/racism-vietnam-war.html.
3 Hallin, Daniel C. *The Uncensored War: The Media and Vietnam*. The California Press, 1989.

CHAPTER 5

1 Berman, Larry. *No Peace, No Honor: Nixon, Kissinger, and Betrayal in Vietnam*. The Free Press, 2002.
2 The American Presidency Project. "Address to the Nation on the War in Vietnam." November 3, 1969. Retrieved from: presidency.ucsb.edu/ws/?pid=2303
3 The American Presidency Project. "Letter to University Student Randy J. Dicks on the 'Vietnam Moratorium.' " October 13, 1969. Retrieved from: presidency.ucsb.edu/ws/index.php?pid=2261.
4 Dunlap, D. "Supreme Court Allows Publication of Pentagon Papers." *The New York Times*, June 30, 2016. Retrieved from: nytimes.com/2016/06/30/insider/1971-supreme-court-allows-publication-of-pentagon-papers.html.
5 Gwertzman, B. "Thieu Aide Discloses Promises of Force by Nixon to Back Pact." *The New York Times*, May 1, 1975. Retrieved from: partners.nytimes.com/library/world/asia/050175vietnam-thieu-bg.html.
6 *Newsweek* Staff. "Last Helicopter Evacuating Saigon." *Newsweek*, April 26, 2015. Retrieved from: newsweek.com/last-helicopter-evacuating-saigon-321254

RESOURCES

INDEX

communist insurgents in, 32, 33, 35, 36–38
Diem's presidency in, vi, 32–33, 36, 38–39, 85
division creating, vi, 23, 31, 32
fall of, 2, 87, 90
resistance of, 2, 5–6. See also Vietnam War
revolution involving, 9–24, 30, 31, 85
U.S. financial aid to, 6, 88, 89, 90, 103
Soviet Union, 2, 4, 5, 17, 19, 20, 21, 22, 26–27, 29, 30, 31, 35, 79
Spring Offensive, 90
Strategic Hamlet Program, 36–38

T

Tet Offensive, vii, 70–72, 83
Thieu, Nguyen Van, 45, 77, 87–89, 90
Tho, Le Duc, vii, 86–88
timeline, vi–vii
Truman, Harry S., vi, 19, 24, 28–29, 85
tunnels, 4, 56, 57

U

United States
aftermath and legacy of war in, 7, 93–97, 99–106
capitalism in, 27
communism opposition by, 2, 5, 19, 20, 23, 26–40, 44–47, 62–63, 77
Declaration of Independence, 24
erosion of public trust in government in, 4, 86, 94, 95
Korean War stance of, 29
Soviet Union conflict with, 2, 4, 5. See also Cold War
Vietnam revolution stance of, 18, 19, 21, 22–23, 85
in Vietnam War (see Vietnam War)

V

veterans, 84, 94, 95, 96–97, 100–102, 105, 106
Vietcong, vi–vii, 33–35, 36–38, 45, 49–50, 52–57, 71–72, 77, 83
Viet Minh, vi, 17–23, 30, 33

Vietnam
aftermath of war in, 94, 97–99, 103–104
communism in, vi, 2, 5, 16, 17, 19, 20, 23, 30–39, 44–45, 62–63, 77, 104
division of, vi, 23, 31, 32. See also North Vietnam; South Vietnam
early history of, vi, 11
economy of, 36, 61, 97, 99, 103–104
French colonization and conflict in, vi, 12–23, 30, 31, 85
geography and map of, 10–11
independence of, vi, 12, 18–19, 20, 23, 24
refugees from, 30, 99
revolution in, history of, 9–24, 30, 31, 85
wars in (see First Indochina War; Vietnam War)
Vietnamization, 77, 80, 83–84
Vietnam Syndrome, 105
Vietnam Veterans Memorial, vii, 101–102, 107
Vietnam War
aftermath and legacy of, 7, 93–106
allies during, 52
antiwar movement, vii, 3, 8, 59–74, 76, 77, 80–82, 84, 86, 100, 105
beginning of, 2, 5–6
bombings during, 33, 46–47, 50, 51, 54, 56, 63, 73, 76, 78–79, 83–84, 87–88, 97
casualties from, vii, 2, 55, 58, 63, 69, 72, 76, 87, 106
Cold War conflicts influencing, 25–39
declaration of war, lack of, 49
defoliation campaign in, 55, 97, 98
draft during, vii, 64–66, 100, 105
Eastertide Offensive in, 86
end of, vii, 2, 76–90
escalation of, 45–50
Ford presidency at end of, vii, 89, 90, 95
fragging incidents in, 83
ground troops during, 50–57, 81
guerrilla warfare in, 3, 53–54, 56, 101

Gulf of Tonkin incident/Resolution, vi, 48–49, 60, 82
historical documentation of, 6–7, 8, 100
Ho Chi Minh Trail in, vi, 33, 34, 50, 55, 56, 83–84
Johnson presidency during, vi–vii, 39, 44–51, 60–62, 64, 67, 69–73, 85, 95
Kissinger's peace talks to end, vii, 86–88
lessons learned from, 105–106
madman theory to end, 78–79
McNamara's plan for, 45–47
media coverage of, 3, 38, 69–70, 72
My Lai Massacre in, vii, 80, 81
Nixon presidency during, vii, 73, 76–84, 85–89, 105
pacification programs in, 55, 83
peace plans to end, 77–78, 80, 83–84, 86–88, 90
Pentagon Papers on, vii, 84–86, 91
post-U.S. withdrawal, 88–90
prisoners of war in, vii, 48, 87, 88, 96, 103
pro-war supporters, 8, 61, 62–63, 76
as proxy war, 5, 6, 7
racial issues in, 3, 65, 67–68
reality of combat in, 52–54, 58
slang in, 53
Spring Offensive in, 90
stalemate in, 55–57
Tet Offensive, vii, 70–72, 83
timeline of, vi–vii
tunnels in, 4, 56, 57
unconventional nature of, 3–4, 101
Vietcong in, vi–vii, 33–35, 36–38, 45, 49–50, 52–57, 71–72, 77, 83
Vietnam's revolution sparking, 9–24, 30, 31, 85
as war of attrition, 51–52, 55
women in, 5, 54

W

Watergate scandal, 85, 89
Westmoreland, William, 50, 51–52, 55–57, 69, 71, 73, 83
whistleblowers, 80, 91–92
women in Vietnam War, 5, 54